M000231483

FREEDOM

FREEDOM

ALCHEMY FOR A VOLUNTARY SOCIETY

by Stephan A. Hoeller

*This publication made possible with
the assistance of the Kern Foundation*

QUEST BOOKS
The Theosophical Publishing House
Wheaton, Ill. U.S.A.
Madras, India/London, England

Copyright 1992 by Stephan Hoeller
A Quest original. First Edition 1992.
All rights reserved. No part of this book may be
reproduced in any manner without written permission
except for quotations embodied in critical articles
or reviews. For additional information write to:

The Theosophical Publishing House
P.O. Box 270
Wheaton, IL 60189-0270

A publication of the Theosophical Publishing House,
a department of the Theosophical Society in America.

Library of Congress Cataloging-in-Publication Data

Hoeller, Stephan A.
   Freedom : alchemy for a voluntary society / Stephan Hoeller.
    p.   cm.
   Includes index.
   ISBN 0-8356-0678-3 : $11.95
   1. Liberty   I. Title.
B105.L45H63   1992
123′.5 — dc20   91-51012
                                              CIP

Dedicated to the captive peoples who have regained their freedom and to those still awaiting their liberation from captivity.

Contents

The natural world, society, the state, the nation and the rest are partial, and their claim to totality is an enslaving lie, which is born of the idolatry of men.

Nicholas Berdyaev
The Beginning and the End

Preface

A devotee of freedom is made, not born. The off-spring of artists, intellectuals or nobility with bohemian sympathies, as in my own case, do not always grow up to be natural libertarians. I came to value freedom because I, along with all my relatives and acquaintances—indeed, my entire nation—were subjected to its loss so radically and painfully. Experience is a teacher whose lessons become part of one's character, of one's very being. Such has been the result of experience in my own life.

I was not yet ten when Hitler's odious shadow fell on my native Hungary, and not yet thirteen when the Soviet armies, amidst blood, pillage and rape, forced their brand of tyranny upon my people. Within the first few days of Soviet occupation, my favorite uncle, an aged invalid, was murdered by soldiers of the Red Army. At the same time, my father miraculously escaped the same fate, after being wounded three times by his would-be executioners. The savagery of Soviet occupation soon was amplified by the oppressions visited upon us by the newly-installed communist regime. No one who has not personally experienced life in a state of constant terror can comprehend the conditions under which we lived. Daily hunger, lack of heat in winter, buildings severely damaged by bombing all paled when compared to the treatment accorded to the populace by its new rulers. I shall never forget the cold, winter morning in 1946, when, upon returning to our temporary home in the hills of Buda, I encountered two small neighbor children wandering bewildered on the street and learned that their parents had been taken away by the secret police, leaving the children orphaned and destitute. Incidents of this sort were a daily occurrence.

My father, one of the always considerable number of Anglophile Hungarian noblemen, spent several years of his early life in England, and was thus a confirmed opponent of Hitler's Germany and a partisan of Britain and America. His sentiments were shared by virtually all of my relatives and friends. Needless to say, the disappointment of all of us with the inability of the Western allies to save us from the clutches of Stalin, into which the treaties of Yalta and Potsdam delivered us, was great. Opponents of Nazism, unless they were communists, were treated as enemies by the new "People's Democracy." My maternal aunt was first imprisoned by the Nazis for harboring Jews on her estate and later imprisoned and tortured by the communist regime as its potential opponent. In some cases, one generation of a family perished in a Nazi concentration camp, while the second was killed by the Soviet occupation forces or by the communist police.

The poet Yeats lamented in the bleak years of the thirties that "the best lack all conviction/while the worst/are full of passionate intensity." With the descent of the deadly, dark cloud of communist tyranny, most of us would have agreed with these words. Still, it was not truly so. While the worst were certainly full of passionate intensity, the best were neither lacking all conviction, nor were they without the courage to express their convictions. Several heroic figures rose on the horizon. The greatest, Joseph, Cardinal Mindszenty, head of the Roman Catholic Church of Hungary, like the brave shepherd he was, fiercely opposed the wolves devouring his flock. For a few, brief months, his voice brought hope to the hopeless. But soon this last and bravest of the resisters was consigned to the dungeons of the secret police, and with him, all hope vanished. A few lucky souls fled to freedom; the rest remained and, for the most part, despaired.

During the years I spent under Soviet occupation, I had numerous conversations with soldiers of the Red Army. The soldiers were young, poor and uninformed. Quite often they would ask earnestly where the poor people lived, for even the most simple hut in a Hungarian village appeared palatial to them. Their commissars had indoctrinated them to believe that people outside the Soviet Union lived in unspeakable poverty, from which only communism could liberate them. Having discovered that they had been deceived, the soldiers often would say that upon their return home, they would take Stalin and his henchmen to task for these lies. Needless to say, such statements were always whispered, lest the ubiquitous secret police (predecessors of the notorious KGB) overhear the conversation. More than once I observed high-ranking army officers fall silent when a common secret policeman passed by. In spite of their barbarous behavior toward them, of which the very high number of rapes were the most humiliating, many Hungarians regarded their conquerors with a measure of pity. Most came to recognize that the oppressors were oppressed themselves, and that the Russian people had been experiencing a long Calvary to which Hungarians were only now being introduced.

After three years under communist rule, I escaped to the West. I was sixteen years old and obliged to leave my parents behind. (Happily they joined me in about a year's time.) In the years that followed, while residing in Belgium, Austria and other Western European countries, I often wondered what would have happened had I stayed in Hungary. Descending from a long line of patriots (my mother's ancestor, Count István Széchényi, is known in history as the greatest Hungarian patriot ever), I felt a sense of guilt for deserting my country in its need. Still, my prospects in the now entrenched communist society were bleak indeed. As a "class alien," I would not qualify for higher education, and virtually any career of a promising nature would be closed to me for the same reason. Within a year of my departure, most of my friends and relatives, along with tens of thousands of upper and middle class "suspicious persons," were forcibly deported from the cities and assigned to menial labor in the countryside, a practice employed during the cultural revolution in China and in the "killing fields" of Cambodia. Exile thus appeared the lesser of evils.

Western Europe in the late forties and early fifties was not a land of milk and honey. There were physical hardships aplenty, and these, added to the pain of homesickness, made life less than pleasant. Still, there was one great boon to be enjoyed: freedom. For the first time in years, free speech, freedom of religion and freedom of assembly were available. It was at this time that I came face-to-face with the reality of how precious freedom can be, once it has been lost and regained.

What did it matter if one lived in cramped refugee quarters, wore shabby clothing and partook of a limited diet? One was free, and that meant much, perhaps everything. Not that the long hand of tyranny did not reach out toward one even under these conditions. The following incident certainly convinced me of that.

One day in 1948 I was invited to one of the offices of the Intelligence Service of the United States occupational forces in Austria. Speaking through an interpreter, the official in charge informed me that the Hungarian communist government had marked me for kidnapping and forcible return to Hungary. He advised me to exercise great care when associating with strangers, especially my own countrymen. I was to report to his office any suspicious circumstances I might become aware of. Gratefully I observed all the rules outlined to me by the American gentleman. It is my firm conviction that this warning saved me from a dire fate. To this day I have a soft spot in my heart for the C.I.A. (now so often attacked) and for its predecessor, the C.I.C. My freedom in exile could have come to an unpleasant end but for these clever agents of the U.S. government!

There was one place where, I felt, freedom was firmly established, and where both people and their freedoms were far safer than they were in Europe. This place was the United States, or as we all called it, America. It is to this country that I came in the early fifties. It was a move I never regretted. Life in the U. S. A. was very different then from what it has become at the end of this twentieth century. The cold war had just begun; an increasing number of Americans became aware that far from making the world safe for democracy, World War II had made much of the world vulnerable to the depredations of a tyranny as fearsome as that of Hitler. Yet many naive notions persisted and caused me consternation whenever I was faced with them.

Having spent their lives under democratic rule, few Americans had a practical appreciation of the realities of authoritarian government. "If the Hungarians don't like the communists, why don't they just vote them out of office?" This was a question I was asked repeatedly. The fact that there was not a single communist government anywhere in the world that had come to power in a free election was totally unknown to these folk. The close similarities between the just vanquished Nazi tyranny and the newly expanding communist power also seemed to elude many. One of the reasons was, no doubt, the natural reluctance to perceive so recent an ally as the Soviet Union as a bloodthirsty enemy. Another was the publicity given to the horrors of Nazi atrocities, especially the holocaust of the Jewish people, which was in no way balanced by an adequate exposure of the Russian gulag and the many other gulags in the satellite countries. I soon recognized that much education and information were required before the American people would fully understand the predicament in which they found themselves in facing the red colossus on the other side of the Atlantic.

As the years wore on, I became aware of certain deep conflicts and conundrums in the American psyche, which I held to be responsible for many of the attitudes I encountered. As a student of Jungian psychology, I came to see that phenomena such as guilt and projection were uncommonly prevalent in the minds of those with whom I held conversations about such issues as freedom, communism and the fate of my homeland. For example, I discerned that the enslavement and discrimination practiced in this country against the population of African origin resulted in much free-floating guilt, which in turn made Americans very sensitive to the issue of racial persecution, but far less sensitive to persecution motivated by class hatred. On the basis of personal experience, I knew that ill treatment and injustice hurt equally whether the target of such indignities is a Jew, an aristocrat or a farmer resisting the collectivization of his plot of land. Often I was shocked by what appeared to me a kind of selective humanitarianism among Americans, but being aware of the psychological dynamics underlying such inconsistencies, I found them easier to bear.

Tout comprendre c'est tout pardonner (to understand all is to forgive all) is a French saying I learned long ago. As my stay in the U. S. lengthened to years and then decades, I was less and less disturbed by the psychological gulf separating me from most Americans. I knew that without experiencing what it means to be deprived of freedoms one has taken for granted, it is exceedingly difficult to understand the predicament of the millions enslaved by political tyrannies. To have faith in someone else's experience is difficult, although there are times when such faith is needed. While growing more philosophical about these issues, I began to be alarmed by others.

My concern was and remains that while I came to my country of exile because it was the freest in the world, I found that a diminishment of freedom was setting in. Freedom was waning in the land of the free, and this phenomenon was not only passively accepted but actively promoted by many. My studies in American history disclosed to me that the founders of this nation envisioned it as a Hermetic vessel, an alchemical alembic in which the human soul could grow and transform with little or no interference from state, society or religious establishments. The existing trends indicated, to my dismay, that interference from just such sources was mounting steadily, and that the intentions of the sage statesmen of old were being increasingly vitiated.

Today, unlike in earlier times, the American people seem to look increasingly to government for the satisfaction of their needs and for the remedy to almost all ills that beset them. In return for the promise of governmental help, they willingly forego numerous freedoms which they previously considered precious. This process often takes the form of one group of people advocating that the freedoms of another group be curtailed, such as persons outside the business and manufacturing community wishing to restrict profits, or special interest groups demanding rights and privileges at the expense of others. Emboldened by the empowerment bestowed upon it by the acquiescence of the people, the government enacts more and more measures which imply the curtailing of freedoms. Laws and ordinances are adopted daily which give little or no consideration to the loss of freedom of individual citizens. Government and people alike fix their sight on their avowed goals and pay little heed to the freedoms which are trampled as the march toward the goal proceeds. Examples of this curious process appear in several chapters that follow. I began to consider that freedom may not always be lost in the same way; sometimes it may be forcibly taken from us from the outside, while at other times, it may simply erode from within. What, I ask, can one do in the face of the latter possibility?

Casting about for kindred views, I came to note that a thoroughgoing concern for freedom did not seem to exist at any point of the current political spectrum. American liberals (and their ideological equivalents in other countries) are concerned with the freedom of the individual, but only when such freedoms fit in with their favorite fads (the latest ones, often summed up under "political correctness," being multiculturalism, feminism and environmentalism). Conservatives show concern for property rights and the rights of business and industry, but tend to favor individual rights only when these do not conflict with dogmas usually derived from the religious right ("right to life," sexual mores, war on drugs and other items covered under a vague umbrella of "Judeo-Christian family values"). Needless to say, neither of these positions could satisfy my libertarian yearnings. I even discovered that there exists a movement, including a political party calling itself "Libertarian," but I found most persons attached to this label to be obsessed with economics, a subject which I consider to be at best but a partial consideration in the debate at hand.

Faced with such disillusionments I decided to put forth some modest efforts of my own directed toward the advocacy of freedom. Within the context of these efforts I availed myself of a certain matrix of psychospiritual thought to which I had been attached for much of my adult life. I am referring to the alternative spirituality of Western culture in its manifestations as Gnosticism, Hermeticism, Theosophy and Jungian psychology. After having expounded some aspects of this spirituality in my lectures and books, I decided to investigate the social application of these teachings with a special view to their relevance to the issue of freedom. The chapters that follow are the result of this investigation.

This book is very different from others I have written. Most of its chapters were delivered in lecture form, and are not free from certain imperfections of style. The content, in turn, may be puzzling to many. Readers interested in Jungian psychology and in alternative spirituality tend toward views which are either apolitical or located on the left of the political spectrum. Most such persons were involved in the remarkable ferment of the sixties when spiritual interests were often conjoined with left-wing political activism. Not many are aware that C. G. Jung was a fierce opponent of Marxism and other totalitarian philosophies, and even fewer know of the savage persecution visited upon theosophical and kindred spiritual groups in communist countries. Liberal religious views often seem to go hand in hand with political liberalism, the latter often amounting to some sort of socialism. Yet it is important to remember that the word *liberal* is derived from the Latin *libertas*, meaning "freedom."

I ask my readers to consider that there is a vital relationship between nonmainstream spirituality and the issue of freedom. I ask for a hearing for a point of view which many may not have previously considered. This point of view always possessed merit, but is even more timely now when the Marxist experiment has proven itself to be a pitiful failure, not only in human terms, but in its political and economic dimensions as well. It is my hope that this book may initiate a rapprochement between libertarian thought and the community of alternative spirituality, including Jungian psychology.

Finally, I wish to express my gratitude to the following: Dr. James C. Ingebretsen for his sustained psychological and practical support given to the writing of this book; Ray Grasse who brought it to the attention of the publisher; Shirley J. Nicholson for her helpful editorial suggestions; Roger Weir who kindly shared with me the results of his pioneering research into Hermetic America; Charles A. Coulombe for friendship, cheer and encouragement; and to others too numerous to mention.

Stephan A. Hoeller
Hollywood, California
January, 1992

Introduction:
The Gnosis of Freedom

The late 1980s and early 1990s have been characterized by a well-nigh miraculous series of events which have freed the peoples of what were once the Soviet Union and its satellite countries from prolonged oppression by the system under which they were forced to live for many decades. The motivating force for these developments was everywhere identical—the desire for freedom. As it has so often in the history of our troubled planet, freedom has become a most vital consideration, an overwhelmingly powerful factor in the affairs of the world. It was not economics, or raising the standard of living, or, for that matter, concern for a clean environment or any of the numerous other issues which have been publicized in recent years that made this large segment of humanity stare down the tanks and guns of their oppressors. Their objective was freedom, pure and simple.

What then is freedom, and why do people time and again risk all for this elusive gift of the gods? What must we do to achieve it, and once achieved, what may we do

1

to secure its presence for us? Many have fought for liberty, equality and fraternity over the last few hundred years, only to be victimized after their victory by new and fearful tyrannies. What then, we must ask, goes wrong so often with humanity's quest for freedom? Why is freedom glimpsed so often only in passing, a reality intimated but often not achieved in any lasting sense?

If we are to answer these questions meaningfully, we must first liberate the idea of freedom from the aura of philosophical abstraction which so frequently surrounds it. Clearly "freedom" does not exist as a sort of Platonic idea by and of itself, but must be understood as manifesting at the existential level in people's lives. C. S. Lewis said that one never experiences a toothache in the abstract, nor eats an abstract meal; rather, one experiences a specific pain and eats a particular meal. In the same manner one might say that freedom is the ability of specific persons to be free from specific restrictions inhibiting their growth, happiness and well-being. Freedom is not a tenuous and elusive set of purely abstract ideas and ideals. When the philosophers of the Enlightenment spoke of "les droits de l'homme" (the rights of man), they meant exactly this: the rights of particular human beings to enjoy concrete personal freedoms.

Once we come to admit that the concept of freedom in general is inextricably bound to the concept of individual freedom, we will soon recognize that we cannot discuss freedom without giving attention to the wider context within which individuals live, move and have their being. Ethics is inevitably grounded in some form of metaphysics, for it is exceedingly difficult to formulate principles for living without a moral scheme or a coherent affirmation of life. If life is meaningless, proceeding from nowhere and having no goal beyond its momentary expression, ethical maxims become useless. Similarly, the liberty of the individual is rendered useless, and therefore lacking in true justification, without some sort of metaphysic—without a meaningful image of the nature, potential and meaning of the life of every individual human being. If we wish to affirm the proposition that freedom is necessary, good or beneficial, we must first ask these basic questions: What is the meaning of the individual? Who and what is the human person? Where do human beings come from and where are they going?

Many people in today's world who have a vital interest in issues of liberty and individuality are asking these questions. The implosion of Soviet power in Central and Eastern Europe has made questions of this nature even more urgent and imperative. The people of Western democratic countries will soon face similar puzzled questions and even accusations from their formerly communist-dominated fellows. Why, they may well ask, do we have no coherent and meaningful set of ideas with which to meet the challenge of other ideologies, or to offer as a replacement for the collectivist and totalitarian ideologies recently discredited? Publicist Irving Kristol defined this predicament cleverly when he wrote that the freedom-loving movement of which he felt himself a part lacked a certain "spinal column" of thought. It seems that the enemies of freedom always have a metaphysic, an internally consistent systematization of values, experience and meaning, while the advocates of freedom have no such support. Tyranny has convictions regarding the meaning of life, but liberty usually has only the existential impact of its own worth. Slavemasters always seem to have an impressive philosophy to justify their power structures of slavery; certainly this was the case with Marxism-Leninism. Countering such ideological arguments, the free can only repeat how good it feels to be free.

Not that freedom-oriented thought is always lacking in ideological underpinnings. First, there are those who are violently opposed to all ideologies, whose opposition itself tends to resemble an ideology all its own. Then, there are what might be called traditionalists, whose allegiance belongs to the mainstream traditions of Judaism and Christianity, often in their orthodox and/or evangelical expressions. These groups' claim to be freedom-loving is open to challenge, however, for much of both Jewish and Christian history is characterized by a lack of regard for personal freedom. If the Jewish-Christian God and his commandments are the true foundations for the rights of humanity, then why have the worshippers and clergy of this God frequently disregarded these rights over the centuries and even millennia? Aside from these and similar arguments, we must recognize that Western society today has a substantial minority which, although spiritually committed, is not part of the mainstream of religious orientation. In the ranks of these people are many whose theoretical and practical regard for freedom is very great. Men and women live in our midst today who are passionately dedicated to freedom, but at the same time fail to agree with the mainstream view—that the Judeo-Christian God is a liberating force in modern society.

This minority includes numerous individuals who have developed an intense interest in and attachment to the modern scientific discipline of depth psychology, often known in its variants of psychoanalysis or analytical psychology. The findings of depth psychology have assumed the status of a philosophy of life for many. Among the outstanding representatives of this discipline, the thought of C. G. Jung is currently receiving mounting sympathetic interest in our culture. Jung was a good example of the modern, creative, intellectual and artistic person; he was profoundly religious, or, we might say, spiritual in his orientation, but he was far removed from the mainstream of traditional religious dogma. Those who choose to investigate his contribution to culture find a synthesis of human knowledge seldom before achieved. Beginning as a physician intent upon curing the ills of the mind, Jung discovered the great truth of the reality of the human psyche, the phenomenology of which he explored. In the deepest strata of the human mind Jung discovered certain previously obscured or unknown forces and images, which are powerfully related to important aspects of culture—myth, religion, art, philosophy and literature. Based on these and related discoveries, Jung developed a number of ideas of a sociological and political character. Since he lived in the era of the two world wars and of Nazi and Communist totalitarianism, Jung naturally came to relate himself powerfully to some of the great social and historical questions of his time, and, indeed, of our time as well.

Looming behind Jung and interwoven with his thought is a school of spirituality which, while often maligned and misunderstood in the past, is once again receiving a good deal of attention. This school is the ancient spiritual philosophy of Gnosticism. Jung was, as some are beginning to discover now, a modern Gnostic. (See my books, *The Gnostic Jung and the Seven Sermons to the Dead*, 1982, and *Jung and the Lost Gospels*, 1989). Within the last twenty years there has been an increasingly powerful and sympathetic interest in the teachings of Gnosticism. The discovery in 1945 and publication in 1977 of the largest archaeological discovery of Gnostic writings and the subsequent literature of commentaries has restored and in fact rehabilitated to a great extent the teachings of the Gnostics. (See *The Nag Hammadi Library*, James Robinson ed., 1977, and *The Gnostic Gospels*, Elaine Pagels, 1979.)

Gnosticism is most frequently regarded as a Christian heresy of the first three centuries A.D., and very few have regarded it as having social or political implications. One exception was the late Austrian emigré scholar Eric Voegelin, who in the 1950s, in such books as *The New Science of Politics*, *Order and History* and others, engaged in much farfetched speculation that Gnosticism was in some obscure way the true ancestor of most of the political ideologies which the author considered iniquitous. Voegelin argued that all the modern totalitarian ideologies were in some way spiritually related to or descended from ancient Gnosticism. He reasoned that since Gnostics had little liking for the Old Testament God, even when represented as God the Father in Christianity, they would not wish to join him in heaven. Thus, they must wish to substitute for such a heaven an earthly Utopia, a heaven on earth. At the same time, Voegelin admitted, the Gnostics regarded the earthly realm as not particularly perfectable. Voegelin never really bothered to clear up this contradiction, and thus his argument was flawed from the beginning. Under the pressure of a more moderate and better informed scholarly climate, enthusiasm for Voegelin has waned considerably in recent decades. For example, scholar and senator Samuel Hayakawa has subjected Voegelin's theories to severe criticism, identifying their author as a sort of academic crank. Disregarding Voegelin's theories, we may find much useful inspiration for contemporary interest in freedom in Gnostic thought, especially in the light of the teachings of Jung.

This book argues that the psychological and spiritual approach to freedom represented by Jung, and before him by the Gnostics, is singularly well-suited to be an ideological support for a contemporary dedication to human freedom. Jung's ideas also buttress the suspicions many of us nourish concerning big government, a controlled economy, the interference of government in the private lives of citizens and the almost inevitable culmination of such conditions in totalitarian tyranny. It may be that for some, the logical positivism and materialistic rationalism of Ayn Rand can serve as satisfactory ideological justifications for a view of life devoted to freedom. It is also within the realm of possibility that for others, especially those who are not bothered by logical or historical inconsistencies, the "Old-Time Religion" of fundamentalism may serve as an adequate basis for a concern for liberty. Still, there are other alternatives. Between born-again Christianity and rationalistic atheism there is a middle ground, where reason and spirit, or as Jung would say, ego and Self, can meet in freedom.

From whatever perspective it may be viewed, from whatever watchtower of the mind or spirit it may be observed, freedom is extremely important. Freedom is precious both as an objective of human efforts and as the means to the achievement of the greatest goals of the human condition. Freedom is also a paradoxical reality, easily lost sight of in the storm of life. Not always is freedom easily discernible. When the German armies paraded into tiny Austria, when Russian tanks rolled into Budapest or Prague, when the workers of Warsaw and Gdansk were herded from their factories into concentration camps by their "socialist" masters, it was not difficult to discover what was meant by freedom. Something definite, something concrete was being taken from its rightful owners. When the heroic members of the Russian parliament defied the might of the troops sent against them by the old-line communist plotters of August, 1991, it was clear where freedom stood and where tyranny could be found.

There are other times when freedom tends to elude us, when the lines are not so clearly drawn. Paradoxical, yet precious is the issue of freedom. When someone greatly in love feels that in the arms of the beloved infinite freedom can be found, but the consummation of the relationship reveals that in lieu of freedom, a new set of tedious human problems have moved into the focus of consciousness, the idea of freedom becomes blurred. Similarly, when idealistic men and women, deeply concerned about issues of human suffering and misery, busy themselves in establishing a welfare state from which they hope the numerous afflictions of living might be banished, but discover instead that the absolute state they have created has destroyed their individuality absolutely, the reality of freedom begins to shimmer and vibrate like a mirage. Freedom, it seems, is the great and precious paradox of our age, or of any age. In this world, though we desire freedom, in our very efforts directed toward realizing our desire, we often become "unfree."

And yet, we must accept the fundamental reality of freedom. The vision of freedom is not an illusion or a mirage. Deeply within us, a voice cries out declaring that in some mysterious way we were indeed "born free," and that it is incumbent upon us to realize our birthright. Now as ever, the pursuit of human freedom is one of the most worthwhile, if not the most worthwhile of all endeavors. May this book aid and amplify that pursuit.

1

Individual Soul Against Mass Mind

One of the most unfortunate circumstances of contemporary life is the degeneration and deterioration of both the concept and the meaning of the word "politics." Aristotle stated with timeless insight that man is a political animal. The word "politics" in its original meaning is derived from the word *polis*, which described the city or city-state of the Greeks. From this key word, the people of the cradle of Western philosophy derived the words *politeia*, translated as "state," and *polites*, meaning "citizen." Even the English word "citizen" contains the word "city," thus calling attention to what may be one of the greatest and most creative cultural archetypes of humanity: *The City*.

The city has been with us for a very long time, and its importance to the growth of human consciousness has been immense. Babylon, Egypt, Greece and Rome have all earned their reputations as the progenitors of Western culture by their having developed cities within which the great alchemy of human progress and transformation could take place. As the alchemists knew that

9

the philosopher's stone and the elixir of life could develop only in a properly designed vessel of great strength, so the peoples of the ancient Mediterranean were aware that cities were needed as vessels of transformation from which might arise such wonders of culture as art, education, religion and philosophy. Cities also made possible the kind of conscious community life which allows free, evolving human beings to live together under conditions conducive to individual and collective spiritual growth.

C. G. Jung, the great knower of the laws and goals of spiritual growth, commented approvingly on a statement popular in religious circles during the Middle Ages, which was probably derived from earlier, pre-Christian sources: *Extra Ecclesiam Nulla Salus*, usually, but somewhat incorrectly translated as, "Outside of the church there is no salvation." Prior to the coming of Christianity, ancient Greeks used the term *ekklesia* to denote the assembly of the electorate, or the constituent membership of the city-state. Jung thus took the statement to mean that in a psychological sense, community, especially community of a particular kind (*ekklesia*, or in its Latin form *ecclesia*) contains a great healing, or saving value (*salus*) for humanity. Thus the statement more correctly means that health, salvation, wholeness (all concepts contained in the word *salus*) are not accessible outside of the context of community.

There is something mysteriously powerful, sacred and mystical about the *ekklesia* or constituency of the city in the classical sense. In the city-state the individual is already differentiated to a considerable degree from the collective or mass mind. The herd instinct has been to a large extent overcome. People are individuals; they have their individual pursuits, their own goals, and purposes. Not only are city-dwellers no longer domi-

nated by the herd instinct, but they are no longer enslaved by nature either. We must remember, especially
today when the shadow side of urbanization has made
many people into romantic worshippers of nature, that
adopting an urban rather than an agricultural lifestyle
has brought great opportunities for the growth of consciousness for many people throughout history. In the
classical sense, the urban lifestyle affords humans the
opportunity to be free of the blind tyranny of nature, its
cycles and laws. In the city human beings become autonomous; in other words, they become their own law-
givers, rather than submitting to the laws of nature. It is
perhaps easy to forget in our days how limiting and
tyrannical the rule of nature can be for human consciousness. Jung has wisely pointed out that nature is
one of the primary symbols of the archetype of the
Great Mother, which in turn is one of the primary symbols of unconsciousness. Nature, and with her, instinctuality, tribalism and herd instinct, are the great carriers of unconsciousness in human life.

As these factors are controlled, human beings become
more conscious, and with consciousness comes autonomy, sovereignty and the ability of the individual to
call on his or her *own* conscious resources of will, decision making, judgment, reason and meaning. While it
would be a mistake to assume that nature, instincts and
collective factors can, or should be repressed and shack-
led in the life of the individual or of the community, we
must realize that it is city-life rather than pastoral or
agricultural life that historically brought the true
growth of consciousness.

The Greek *polis*, the city, and its community, the *ekklesia*, were therefore uniquely archetypal and creative
developments in the life of humanity. For the first time
in history, free individuals began to be involved in the

political process by taking an active and responsible part in governing themselves. The views expressed by Plato and other leading thinkers regarding forms of government have a profound bearing on the psychological overtones of this political process. Of the three forms of government known to the Greeks, democracy, aristocracy and tyranny, the philosophers tended to prefer aristocracy, because in their view it represented the rule of the best, (most conscious) persons, the *aristoi*, who would obviously govern in accordance with the enlightened dictates of consciousness. Direct democracy appeared as too hazardous to the wise men of classical antiquity. They felt it might easily lend itself to mob-rule, or to similar regressions to the instinctuality of the herd. Thus the Greeks were responsible for the unique and valuable concept of using the political process for enhancing the consciousness of individuals. Politics, in the classical Greek understanding of its meaning, was really *a phenomenon of psychological individuation.*

Politics as the Vehicle of Consciousness

It is clear that politics can and indeed should be something radically different from what it has become in the contemporary mind and society. Politics, the science of community, is in a certain sense also an expression of the science of the soul and of the art of the soul's growth and transformation. The life of the community can become a useful modality for the enhancement, amplification and expansion of individual consciousness. In contemporary society, this is seldom the case, but this regrettable circumstance by no means mitigates against the fact that the political process can have such spiritual value, and that there were times when this value was openly recognized and cultivated.

Both Jung and the Gnostic wisdom can shed a considerable light on the value of politics. The Gnostics were culturally Greek, having lived and worked in the so-called Hellenistic period of antiquity, within which the Greek spirit, amplified and enriched by other cultural influences, acted as a magnificent synthesizing agent of spiritual currents. The very word *gnostikos* "knower" is, of course, Greek. The Greeks called certain persons, whom they suspected of unusual acumen in spiritual matters, *gnostikoi*, or "people who know." From our point of view, we might say that the Gnostics were individuated persons, or technicians of individuation. Such persons would as a matter of course have a great, even an overweening concern with freedom, and the Gnostics definitely had such a concern.

Conforming to the prevailing genre, the Gnostics did not express their concerns with liberty in simple political or declarative terms, but rather employed myth and poetic imagery to give voice to their ideals and preoccupations. Their central myth, which to them was no mere fable, but a matter of profound spiritual dedication, depicted the existential need of the soul to free itself from the shackles and limitations of its condition in the world. An important role in this myth was played by the figures of *demiurgoi* and *archontes*. These were envisioned as cosmic-psychological tyrants and oppressors of the soul, whose natural tendency predisposed them to an inimical attitude toward human liberty, spiritual or physical. Gnostics saw themselves as the vanguard of human freedom, struggling by the use of spiritual means against the ubiquitous forces of tyranny in the realms of nature and being. The Gnostic preoccupation with the issue of liberty led to the much debated and maligned position of antinomianism, which means opposition to rigid structures of religious legalism (*anti* means "against"; *nomos* means "law"). The

Gnostic approach to religion was and is highly individualistic and nonconformist. All in all, it would be quite correct to say that Gnostics throughout history were spiritual libertarians. Of course, this libertarianism proved to be their downfall. The Gnostics were not organized in an authoritarian fashion and thus had no effective power structures. Thus they were overwhelmed by forces that possessed the power they themselves lacked—the authoritarian, organized orthodoxy of the newly streamlined Constantinian church, supported by the mightiest power structure of ancient history, Imperial Rome. In more ways than one, Gnosis and Gnosticism were intimately connected with the ideals of a spiritually based political freedom. The Gnostic schools were, in fact, the last vestiges of such freedom when they were obliterated in the third and fourth centuries.

Jung's Modern Gnosis

C. G. Jung, whose modern Gnosis used a psychological modality for its expression, enunciated libertarian principles in essential agreement with and in continuation of the Gnosis of old. Though his was a psychological Gnosis, it was a Gnosis nevertheless. Jung's teachings contain the theme that the soul has an inherent tendency toward individuation, a process whose objective is ultimate wholeness, sovereignty, freedom and autonomy. The process of individuation, according to Jung, consists to a large extent of the union of the opposites in the psyche. High and low, masculine and feminine, good and evil must eventually be reconciled in the souls of human beings. The union of these opposites, moreover, always involves liberating the shadow, bringing the darkness to light within oneself, which is to a great extent an antinomian Gnostic principle. Jung's psychology is in essence about freedom, liberty and liberation, or the increase of freedom. Psychologically, this means freedom from complexes, from thralldom to the unconscious; from one-sidedness of consciousness and from excessive attachment of the conscious ego to itself and to its values and beliefs. Though Jung's is a psychological libertarianism while the Gnostics espoused a religious-spiritual libertarianism, both positions have a definite social meaning, with definable and recognizable political and social implications. To discover some of these and to apply them within a contemporary context is the objective of this chapter and of those which follow. To begin, I explore some of the most important Gnostic ideas, contained in contemporary form in Jung's teachings, which might help illuminate the concept of freedom.

The Conflict of the Individual with the Mass

The first and most important of these ideas is the conflict between the individual human psyche, or the individuating psyche, with the mass psyche, or as it may be called, the conflict of the individual with the mass. We live today in a world very different from the Greek city-states. Ours is for the most part a mass culture, where quantitative cultural factors predominate. Populations are huge, cities gigantic, and conflicts and problems exist on a mass scale. The psychological implications of this condition are considerable and perilous, because under such circumstances, problems take on an overwhelming aspect and may crush the individual. Modern problems tend to become so big that individuals tend to give up and not do anything about them. We must remember to select problems that are our size. To become too global, too cosmic in our thinking about problems is always fatal. We must keep our problems small, so that we may be able to do something about them.

Still, it must be kept in mind that mass-mindedness is not just the result of a world in which many things exist on a mass or huge scale. Jung said that there was a definite historical process that produced the modern mass mind. Political and social theories and practices do not exist in a philosophical and psychological vacuum; they are organically linked to two important factors: (1) the human being's view of the universe, and (2) the human being's view of himself or herself. A concept of society, government and justice always rests on a cosmo-conception and on a view of soul redemption. These two conceptions may not always be consciously verbalized, but they are nevertheless always present. Thus behind every political and social condition is both a metaphysics and a metapsychology.

To illustrate, it may be useful to recall a few examples. Behind feudalism and the premercantile and prefinancial character of medieval society stood the Augustinian Christian *Civitas Dei*, the concept of a transcendentally inspired "godly" society. Similarly, for the first one hundred and fifty years of its history, the United States based its political and socioeconomic practice on the ideas and ideals of the Age of Enlightenment, with its essential belief in the perfectibility of human beings. This basis made economic laissez faire, free enterprise and various forms of individualism appear to be the necessary outflow of these ideals. On the opposite pole, National Socialist (Nazi) Germany and its many horrors were not *sui generis,* or the mere expression of the insane will of a clique of madmen. Rather, behind the Nazi horror loomed a ruthless mythos, no less impressive for being befuddled, of blood and soil and the metaphysical sacredness of race. Similarly, Communist Russia and its satellites (including Mao's China, and the Asian Communist dictatorships) were or are rooted respectively in a dogmatic worldview, derived from Marx and Engels and having distinctly metaphysical overtones.

Western culture has been based for some twelve to thirteen hundred years on the Christian ecclesiastical worldview. Its dominance may be reckoned roughly to have endured from 400 A.D. to 1600 A.D. This worldview was by no means a perfect ideology; it had powerful repressions built into its fabric, as Jung pointed out, particularly against nature, sex and the creative imagination. It was a worldview characterized by a considerable amount of unconsciousness; and the culture based upon it was cruel, violent and superstitious, but it held together for a long time. The political and ethical system of this ideology and society was effective and had considerable staying power. Then the structure began to crumble. The first blow came from science, or more precisely from the science of astronomy. Nicolaus Copernicus, Galileo Galilei and Johannes Kepler challenged the Ptolemaic system of geocentric astronomy, thereby assailing the symbolic structure of the traditional conception of the Christian cosmos. The next attack was made by Niccolo Machiavelli in the field of statecraft, when he declared that no conventional rules of morality were to bind the ruler of a country. Thus the heavens and the princes both became exempt from the conditions of the medieval Christian law of the cosmos. Then came the Reformation of Luther and Calvin, who divided the previously monolithic fabric of the Church itself. These influences were followed by those of the science of physics, in which Isaac Newton exempted the microcosm of the physical world from direct divine guidance and governance.

The Enlightenment drove the medieval theological cosmology more or less successfully out of philosophy and literature: Voltaire, Rousseau, and their fellows accomplished a secularization of intellectual and artistic culture that would have appeared impossible a few hundred years earlier. The next move was made by the Industrial Revolution which exempted the field of economics from the ethical structure of traditional Christianity. Then Charles Darwin's evolutionary theory invaded the biological sphere, the very body of the human being, and excluded from this vital area the hand of the Christian Creator Deity. And finally, at the beginning of the twentieth century, psychology, led by Sigmund Freud, drove the coup de grace home by proving, at least to the satisfaction of millions, that there is no divine mystery, no beautiful romantic spark in the soul. Instead, the mind or soul is the dwelling place of fierce lusts and dark complexes and of strange figures, such as the id, the libido and the superego. So it came to pass that the old cosmology was driven from the cosmos, from politics, from the body of the Church through schism, from philosophy, from physics, from biology, from economics and eventually from the last stronghold of religious and spiritual realities, the very soul of the human being. These historical developments have produced two consequences: (1) They destroyed the dominance over Western culture of the Christian cosmology formulated in late antiquity and formalized in medieval times; and (2) they have caused great and grave psychological dislocations, which led to what Jung recognized as the mass mind in contemporary culture.

Several factors thus contributed to the rise of the mass mind:

a) The Reformation emancipated the state from the supernaturally based rule of the Church and gave the state more totalitarian power than it possessed previously.

b) The Enlightenment brought an overemphasis on rationalism and led to a frightful repression of the irrational, unconscious side of the psyche.

c) The Enlightenment and the Industrial Revolution together brought an increasingly alienated individualism, egotism, selfishness and lack of relatedness to the collective factors of life. This, as Jung pointed out, brought a "compensatory reversion to the collective man" in the form of the rise of socialism and communism.

d) The removal of the state and of government from the context of a morally binding religious cosmology bestowed more and more power upon political establishments, and thus Nietzsche's "will-to-power" could increasingly create unrestrained totalitarian societies, with dictatorships of many kinds. Some became conjoined with the "compensatory reversion to the collective man," such as Hitler's National Socialist state and the so-called people's democracies and related dictatorial regimes of Communist countries.

e) The irruption of Freudian ideas into the field of education and sociology has attempted to subject many personal and social phenomena to a cold, rationalistic view, which evaluates human beings in terms of such abstractions as socialization, adjustment, infantilism and narcissism. These concepts contributed greatly to the loss of individual dignity, self-esteem, optimism and creativity. These influences have also contributed to the lowering of the standards of education with a corresponding deterioration of both the intellectual skills and the personal integrity and discipline of those educated by this system. The lower circles of the inferno of modern society have been thus populated by an educational process that has lost its own soul.

All of these phenomena have produced a new creature with what Jung called the "mass psyche." What kind of creature is this? Here are some of the characteristics mentioned by Jung: A person with a mass psyche is socially isolated from other human beings, separated from the unconscious and not in touch with the instincts. Moreover, this person is spiritually uprooted, having no vital connection with symbol systems and authentic traditions of a religious-mystical nature. Such a person is aesthetically insensitive, having little appreciation of beauty either in nature or in art, and is lacking in a sense of romance and imagination to see beyond the personal concerns of the ego. Finally, the mass-minded person expects economic and political changes and upheavals to solve all problems and perplexities, because he or she seeks for the source of all good and evil in the objective environment rather than in subtle, interior factors. Jung said once that he was tempted "to construct a political theory of neurosis, in so far as the man of today is chiefly excited by his political passions."

We have then in the person with a mass psyche a new kind of political animal, very much inferior to the *zoon politikon* of the ancients. The citizen of the ancient city-state made use of the public cause (*res publica* or republic) in a conscious manner to advance the process of individuation, while the modern person with a mass psyche misuses politics as an unrealistic extraverted projection and an occasion for living out the pressures and evils of the unconscious. It is here that human beings become increasingly involved in mass-mindedness. They take to collective and political movements wherein their already precarious and puny individuality dwindles to minuscule proportions. Imitation, dependence, lack of personal judgment, a lowering of the mental level are the inevitable accompaniment of the submerging of the individual in a mass movement. Political mass movements are the great carriers of mass-mindedness, and as such they are, above all, a moral danger. The morality of a group or movement exists in inverse ratio to its size. Jung said that any large company composed of wholly admirable persons has the morality and intelligence of an unwieldy, stupid and violent animal, and that the bigger the organization, the more unavoidable is its immorality and blind stupidity. As the Romans (who had a wise saying for every occasion), used to say: *Senatus bestia, senatores boni viri*, ("The senate is a monster, but the senators are good men").

What then is the answer to the great problem of mass-mindedness? It is evident from the foregoing discussion that the answer will not be found in ideologies and even less in movements, no matter how commendable their proclaimed objectives. The answer is not a movement, but the individual. The individual is the only hope, and since even the mass-minded person is latently an individual, this is a hope of considerable magnitude and promise.

Jung's Gnosis of Hope

The social and historical message of the Gnosis of Jung is one of hope, based on a principle within the innermost soul of every person—the Self, the hope of glory. What really happens in history happens not at the conference tables, not on the battlefields, or on the barricades, but *within us.* C. G. Jung put it this way:

> When we consider the history of humanity, we see only the very surface of events and even these are warped by the dim mirror of tradition. What really happened escapes historical research, for the real historic happening is deeply hidden, lived by all and perceived by none. It is the most private, the most subjective, psychic life and experience. Wars, dynasties, social revolutions, conquests, and religions are all the most superficial symptoms of a secret psychic fundamental attitude in the individual, unknown to him and therefore not recorded by any chronicler. The great events of world history are in themselves of small importance. What is important in the final reckoning is only the subjective life of the individual. In our most private and subjective lives, we are not only these who suffer but also those who make the age. Our age—it is ourselves.
>
> "The Meaning of Psychology for Modern Man"
> in *Civilization in Transition*

This Gnostic, or internalist position is relatively easy to understand and even to agree with, but to draw the proper conclusions from it is rather more difficult. On one hand, we must recognize that it is futile as well as inaccurate to employ negative projection in social and historical matters. Faultfinding is almost always a matter of negative projection. If I feel bad, helpless, depressed, anguished, lacking in ego strength and so forth, I will not be substantially better off if I blame "them" for my condition, whoever "they" may be. No poor man or woman has become richer by raging against the wealthy; no son or daughter with a weak ego has become strong by blaming and denigrating an overbearing mother or an overly stern father. Projecting our negative conditions unto others creates the illusion of improvement, but it is actually an unhealthy mechanism through which we try to make ourselves feel better. The awakening, however, is always harsh, painful and depressing, rather like a severe hangover after an unwise indulgence.

While negative projections prove themselves to be of little value, they often attach themselves to outward causes and charge them with great power. This phenomenon, which has been the bane of ideologies throughout history, is ultimately self-defeating and dangerous to society and individual alike. Jung expresses this idea as follows:

> When a problem that is at bottom personal, and therefore apparently subjective, impinges upon outer events which contain the same psychological elements as the personal conflict, it is suddenly transformed into a general question that embraces the whole of society. In this way the personal problem gains a dignity that was hitherto wanting, since a state of inner discord has an almost mortifying and degrading quality, so that one sinks into a humiliated condition both without and within, like a state dishonored by civil war. It is this that makes one shrink from displaying before a larger public a purely personal conflict, provided, of course, that one does not suffer from an over-daring self-esteem. But when it happens that the connection between the personal problem and the larger contemporary events is discerned and understood, a relativity is established that promises release from the isolation of the purely personal; in other words, the subjective problem is amplified to the dimensions of a general question of our society.
>
> *Psychological Types*

As a rule, such amplification produces more problems than it solves. When personal neuroses are compounded into social and political causes, they do not lose their neurotic character; they just grow from personal neuroses into mass neuroses. From a private problem, they become a general madness. This principle, simple as it is, is one of the most frequently overlooked facts of life, and therefore the cause of the greatest disasters in history. To quote Jung again:

> It is so much easier to preach the universal panacea to everybody else than to take it oneself—and, as we all know, things are never so bad when everybody is in the same boat. No doubts can exist in the herd; the bigger the crowds the better the truth—and the greater the catastrophe.
>
> *Psychology and Alchemy*

The psychologically wise attitude therefore must be one which is invariably distrustful of situations which can lead to mass neurosis or herdlike behavior, in short, to all those blandishments of the collective which usurp the judgment and discrimination of the individual.

Each and every person must become his or her own movement, a personal and unique activist unit, an individual political party. Only ceaseless vigilance in the face of the enticements and temptations of the collective unit will keep us free from mass-mindedness. Jung mentions in this respect the comic example of one of his friends. Jung once found himself with this friend in a huge crowd of people. His friend could take the crowd for only so long; then he suddenly exclaimed, "Here you have the most convincing reason for not believing in immortality; *all those people* want to be immortal!" On the other hand, it is obvious that intelligent and useful changes and transformations must occur in society, or as one might phrase it, social progress is desirable. Can such progress occur without movements, collective causes and their attendant problems? Jung apparently believed that such progress could be accomplished with a minimal involvement of individuals in collective ideologies and causes:

> Our blight is ideologies—they are the long-expected antichrist! Inasmuch as collectivities are mere accumulations of individuals, their problems are also accumulations of individual problems. One set of people identifies itself with the superior man and cannot descend, and the other set identifies itself with the inferior man and wants to reach the surface. Such problems are never solved by legislation and tricks. They are only solved by a general change of attitude. And the change does not begin with propaganda and mass meetings and violence. It begins with a change in individuals. It will continue as a transformation of their personal likes and dislikes, of their outlook on life and their values, and only the accumulation of such individual changes will produce a collective solution.
>
> *Psychology and Religion, West and East*

What is needed then in order to produce social progress is the integrative process of the individual. The elixir of human history is not political, social or even religious ideology with its movements, parties, organizations and churches, but the psychic life of the individual, with its growth and integration, its becoming whole and complete. (It must be noted with satisfaction, that political life in the United States has been historically remarkably free from ideology. When, as it has been the case so often in America, the political process becomes a practical matter of problem solving and of pragmatic exigencies, even though the game of the adversary relationship of political parties is played, the danger of mass-mindedness is minimized, and personal growth within the political process is rendered more likely. Still, the temptation of fanaticism, of "crusades" and quasi-and pseudo-religious influences in politics, among which the secular messianism of Marxism stands out most prominently, is ever present and must be combated. Regrettably, Marxist-influenced ideological elements have not vanished from American society, although they tend to avoid the Marxist label.)

Collective experiences of the psyche are no substitute for the individual experience of transformation. Not only are they not able to take its place, but very often they are inimical to it, because they lower the level of conscious awareness of the individual. As Jung cogently expressed it:

> If I undergo what is called a communal experience within the group, this occurs at a deeper level of consciousness than when I experience something alone. Therefore the group-experience is much more frequent than an individual experience of transformation. It is also much easier to achieve, for the collective presence of many people has a great suggestive power. The individual within the mass is extremely suggestible. As soon as he becomes part of the mass, man is below his usual level. Of course he can retain the memory of the ethically superior being he once was, but when he is in the mass this memory is no more than an illusion. It suffices for something to happen, for instance, a proposal is made which the whole mass adopts, and he is also for it even if the proposal is immoral. Within the mass man feels no sense of responsibility, but also no fear.
>
> *Two Essays on Analytical Psychology*

This truth may be somewhat difficult to appreciate within the context of American culture, with its historically high regard for majority rule and democracy. What we must remember is that the true philosophical foundations of the American system never contained the notion that the majority is always right morally, or that it is philosophically correct and infallible.

Majorities can be wrong, and strong safeguards must at all times exist in order to guard against the potential excesses of majorities. Tyranny exercised by a majority is still tyranny, and often a more dreadful tyranny than one exercised by a minority, which is bound to crumble in some manner eventually. Even though this principle is self-evident in many ways—witness such injustices as lynch laws and the oppression of racial and religious minorities by majorities—a sort of false mythos about the virtues of majority positions has nevertheless infiltrated the thinking of democracies. The acceptance of the lowest common denominator as normative in many areas of life, particularly in education, aesthetics, art and related fields, and a consequent anti-intellectualism and exaltation of vulgarity and intellectual and ethical shabbiness are common phenomena in our culture. All too often we have forgotten that democracy does not imply that the majority position is automatically true or morally right. On the contrary, democracy implies that persons dare to be individuals, even against the prevailing opinions of the majority, if the individual's conscience so dictates.

Individual Transformation and Social Benefit

One of the most important questions still remains unanswered, however. If an individual process of transformation is possible and desirable, how is this transformative process to take place within history, and how can it or will it benefit the structure of society? In other words, if we continue to advance in our internal, and personal transformation, will the world become better?

To answer this question is extremely difficult. Much hinges on the interpretation in this context of the term "better." What do we mean by better? Whose definition of good shall we accept when evaluating betterment or improvement in society? From the point of view of Gnosticism and of its modern manifestation in the views of Jung, true improvement in any condition must include both of the opposite factors which make up the fabric of the matter at hand. Improvement, or progress, therefore, does not imply the gradual vanishing and eventual absence of evil or of conflict, and the steady increase of what one may call good. Against the different varieties of Utopianism, both past and present, Jung and the Gnosis represent a view which strives for wholeness rather than conventional goodness (see Chapter 6 for further material on Utopia). To make society better does not necessarily involve linear improvement of the ordinary variety.

The veracity of this proposition and view is, once again, easily discernible in theory, but becomes beclouded by emotional attitudes and reactions in the arena of practical action. In order to see real improvement in society, it is often necessary for the shadow side of life to emerge into plain view instead of subsisting in the dark recesses of repression and neglect. Many examples could be cited. The racial question certainly was and is in need of recognition and attention, and only by way of its often unpalatable emergence into plain view can proper solutions to its grave problems be developed. The profligate and improvident ways of Communist states, as well as of many third world socialist states could only be halted by measures which did not improve the economy or the quality of life of numerous citizens. In the body politic as well as in the psyche of the individual, the acceptance of the dark shadow often brings turbulence and unhappiness; things have to become worse before they can become better. Implicit in this statement of popular wisdom is the recognition that good and bad, or better and worse, are complementary opposites which only together produce true improvement.

These recognitions are of crucial importance to society. As we discover that society must give positive recognition not only to the so-called good, but also to evil, our body politic may in effect become an alchemical vessel of ultimate transformation. Perhaps what we shall have eventually will not be a better society, but a more complete one, that ceases to repress its own shadow-side, and instead gives it due recognition—hopefully without becoming possessed by it. In this eventuality, society will cease to be the oppressive master of its members; rather it will become the expression of the plurality of the individuals who are the constituent members of its *ekklesia*. We need not fear that society will disintegrate, become decadent or otherwise suffer as the result of such developments. For what or who is society but ourselves? Where did we ever acquire the preposterous notion that society is some sort of self-existing entity, having a life and a meaning apart from the life and meaning of its constituent members? Jung stated the matter most clearly:

> If man cannot exist without society, neither can he exist without oxygen, water, albumen, fat, and so on. Like these, society is one of the necessary conditions of his existence. It would be ludicrous to maintain that man exists in order to breathe air. It is equally ludicrous to say that man exists for the sake of society. "Society" is nothing more than the concept of the symbiosis of a group of human beings. A concept is not a carrier of life. The sole and natural carrier of life is the individual, and this holds true throughout nature.
>
> "Psychotherapy Today" in
> *The Practice of Psychotherapy*

Let us take courage. The present rapid transformation in Western society may spell the end of the baneful philosophy of the excluded middle, which ever prevents the union of the opposites. It is true that many undesirable conditions exist in our society, and that some of these have increased dramatically in recent years and decades. Crime is rampant, and life is less safe than it was some time ago. The once sacrosanct images of family and home are tarnished. The moral shibboleths of the past carry less weight than they did. Poverty and sickness, physical and psychological afflictions are prevalent. Still, there is no reason to suppose that these signs of the times carry overtones beyond their immediate, practical import. They are not signs in the heavens, plagues of Egypt, or heralds of doom or of an apocalyptic future. On the contrary, they indicate that many shadows, previously imprisoned in the Tartarean underworld of civilization now walk in the daylight, where we may see them and understand them. Meaning has ever come forth from conflict and struggle, and the only true peace has always been the peace of the graveyard.

The greatest danger facing our culture and society is not crime, moral decline, poverty or even the much touted factors of pollution and ecological imbalance. Rather it is the insidious but deadly phenomenon of mass-mindedness. If we can combat this danger and keep it at bay, then we may be assured that the potential of a creative and transformative future can be ours. If we lose to this enemy, our options for future changes and progress are few indeed. As long as we continue to resist mass-mindedness, as long as we persist in saying no to turbulent collective movements of one kind or another, there may be rightly nourished within us the merciful hope that the alchemy of history will produce through us and in us the philosopher's stone, the great elixir, the archetype of wholeness, which is the creative union of the opposites. Indeed, these are the times when

we may all say in our own behalf what Jung said after
World War II, "Whereas I formerly believed it to be my
bounden duty to call other persons to order, I now admit that I need calling to order myself."

Let us then call ourselves to order, and we may be
assured that history and the world will answer such a
call. Let us call ourselves to order, which means to call
ourselves to wholeness. The ancient Gnostics said that a
man of light lights up the whole world. C. G. Jung
stated that the individual is the makeweight that tips
the scales of history. We are the individual make-
weights ourselves, and thus the responsibility rests on
us. As Buddha said "Ye suffer from yourselves." And to
the extent that this personal, yet universal burden can
be assumed and carried by us, to that extent have we
been good alchemists, effective masters of the great Art,
and accomplishers of the union of the opposites. It is
then and thus that in the words of poet T. S. Eliot we
shall know:

> And all shall be well;
> And all manner of thing shall be well.
> When the tongues of flame are in-folded
> Into the crowned knot of life,
> And the fire and the rose are one.

2

Old-Time Religion in
Modern Society

Time and again in history we find crusades afoot,
which act on the assumption that the public life of the
culture has moved too far away from the moral precepts
to which a number of citizens pay allegiance. In our
days we are once again confronted with such crusades,
reinforced by the contemporary means of mass persua-
sion, the public media. Vocal minorities of several kinds
seem bent upon exerting pressure on the political sector
of the country. Among these are groups whose professed
motivations are religious and whose program involves
making the general citizenry conform to the moral ideal
which these groups consider to be correct in light of
their own religious convictions.

From the depth psychological point of view, it seems
that we are faced here with more than a mundane issue
of contemporary public life. Rather the activities of
these minorities present a psychological and, in fact, a
spiritual problem which merits our deepest concern.
This chapter considers this set of temporal, public

phenomena within a larger spiritual context, which involves not only the immediate psychological overtones of the present, but which leads as well to the contemplation of a much larger psycho-historical context.

First we must address the relationship of religion to the body politic or to social and public concerns in general. Religion may be defined as the effort of the individual human psyche to link itself up with its greater psychic background, to connect itself with spiritual and archetypal realities within its own deeper mind, indeed within the deeper mind of humanity, and thereby to facilitate a state of wholeness or totality arising within the psyche itself. This definition calls to mind the origins of the word "religion"; it comes from the Latin terms *re*, meaning "back or together," and *ligere*, meaning "to join." Religion comes from the same root as "ligament," which in biology is designed to join things together. Thus by definition, religion has to do with joining the individual soul to its background within a greater reality. We might also say, I think, in a historical perspective, that for better or for worse, religion has always played an enormously important role in human society. For this reason, a historical, or rather psycho-historical survey of the development of human consciousness can be very helpful here. Within such a survey we can discover the authentic character, the roots and the nature of our present situation. For the purpose of this analysis, I shall employ a scheme of development derived from the Jungian writer Erich Neumann, expressed in his works *The Origin and History of Consciousness* and *The Great Mother*. Neumann's developmental scheme is useful in this instance primarily because it helps uncover the relationship between religion and the political life of societies.

Phases of the Growth of Psyche and Society

According to Neumann, certain phases denote the development of consciousness, or more properly, the growth of consciousness. The first phase or stage has been linked symbolically with the figure of the Ourobouros serpent or dragon, a tail-swallowing amphibian. This symbol represents the condition of original totality and self-containment which exists before the birth of consciousness or of the conscious ego. While development is in this phase, the ego exists only as a latent potentiality and is still identical with the totality of the objective psyche. Conscious and unconscious, ego and Self, masculine and feminine are still one in this condition. In the individual, this state is presumed to exist during the prenatal period and in early infancy.

Now let us look at this phase, for our purposes, in politico-religious terms. The equivalent of the primordial, archaic unconsciousness of the embryo, or of the very small infant, would be primitive society. In primitive society, the individual and the collective are still one. The tribe, clan or extended family is both religious and secular in character. Chiefs and kings are often divine, or at least rule by divine right. All of life is religious or sacred in nature. The religious and the secular are not only unified, but not even the faintest concept exists that the two could be envisioned as different. All human acts—drinking, eating, sex, hunting, fighting—are sacred acts. Nothing is profane or mundane; everything is charged with great archetypal import and force. In such a society, the gods live through the human being, their communion with the human is so close and intimate. To speak of individual freedom under these circumstances is nonsensical, because there is no individual to be free. Archaic society is the individual's real self. Society and self are one, and without society, the individual perishes, just like an amputated limb dies when removed from the vitalizing system of the organism. Much of this description pertains also to slightly more developed forms of primitive society.

A good illustration of this phase of society can be found in the ideas of the great humanitarian Dr. Albert Schweitzer. He thought that modern hospital conditions were potentially alienating and psychologically harmful to the African natives to whom he extended his medical ministrations. Instead of isolating the sick patient and putting him or her into a hospital bed in a room alone or with strangers, Schweitzer allowed patients to move into his hospital with their families and their pets and domestic animals, including dogs, chickens, pigs and the like. Needless to say, this arrangement did not enhance the hygienic conditions and the orderliness of the hospital, but it provided the African the kind of psychological support system without which he or she would not have improved physically and would assuredly have perished for psychological reasons. Schweitzer knew that a member of an undifferentiated society cannot survive psychologically outside the bosom of that society. The reality of personhood with its consequent sense of autonomy and self-sufficiency is simply not present in archaic societies.

Lest we become prideful and inflated when comparing ourselves to members of such societies, we must remember that in spite of our modern, civilized alienation, we are still very much partakers of conditions which, at a subtle level, resemble those of the primitive. Psychological support systems of a collective nature are still desirable, although we are no longer dependent on them to such an enormous degree as we once were.

The cardinal feature of the primitive society we are describing is lack of differentiation. Just as the individual is not differentiated from the collective, the secular is not differentiated from the religious. The two are still one. While it is easy for us to infer the shortcomings of such a condition, we must not forget that the unification of these powerful forces also gives the people within such a society considerable psychological power or psychic energy. What it does not give them, however, is individual consciousness, since it is a pre-egoic phase of the development. Although this phase is archaic, there are, in fact, many societies in the present world where this condition still prevails. Moreover, we need to remember that we moderns still carry within us the ancient memory of this condition; consequently, we are not entirely removed from it ourselves. We hanker for it, as it were, on an unconscious level, even as we have an unconscious desire to return, not perhaps to the physical womb of our mothers, as some reductionistic psychologists claim, but rather to the womb of the unconscious. Somehow in the background of all human thinking and feeling is the recognition that there was a time—maybe a time before time—when we were one: when the sacred and the secular were not separate; when every meal was a holy communion; when every act of life was a sacred ritual; when we dwelt within the all-enfolding, all-nourishing and all-sustaining energy system of a great totality, a great ineffable wholeness, and experienced a wonderful feeling of energy, wholeness, protectedness and oneness. The farther we move away from that ancient condition, the greater the longing, the nostalgia to return to a state of that sort.

The Childhood of Consciousness

The next phase to consider is the infancy and childhood of consciousness. Within this epoch consciousness is born, but like most newborn beings, it is very weak. Consciousness at this stage is dim, fitful, sporadic in its expression. An analogy that offers itself is that of a tiny, flickering flame in a large, dark space, that is easily reduced to an imperceptible speck of light or even extinguished by a gust of air. The light of newborn consciousness is rather as if one were to take a little oil lamp out onto a wind-swept and foggy heath, where the gusts may make it appear as if the little flame has been completely put out, until, after the wind subsides, it flames up again. At the level of the growth of individual consciousness, this stage is usually equated with childhood. Human infants and children, unlike most animals, are helpless for a long time. Young children are dependent on the caring ministrations of their mothers in particular. Without mothers, children would perish. This is true psychologically as well as physically.

In psychological terms, we might say that the unconscious, which is the psychic mother, remains in close touch with the child, nourishes it, supports it and influences it. Therefore, children are very close to their unconscious, much closer than adults. For this reason, children are in very close touch with their dreams; they also have a sense of reality about their fantasies that adults do not have. By way of their unconscious in its collective aspect, children are also in some kind of telepathic communication with the unconscious of their parents and appear to partake of it at times. That is why Jung has pointed out that parents ought to realize that not only their conscious and overt acts, but also their unconscious can influence their children. So, let us say, parents may discipline themselves not to argue or show hostility or outbursts of temper in front of their children, but if they have a lot of hostility and anger or disturbance within their psyches, and if they are around their children, the children are likely to be affected by even unexpressed anger. It is not necessary to perform dramatic, overt acts in front of a child in order for the child to get the point. Children are in such close contact with the Great Mother Unconscious that the unconscious of their physical parents is accessible to them.

As we look at this phase of development in social, political and religious terms, we find that in this stage, society, religion and politics, like the ego and the Self, are beginning to separate, but only barely. No secular society, of any kind exists as yet. Priesthood, at this point frequently a feminine priesthood, is supreme. The gods are no longer identified with the priest-kings as they were before, although some divine kingship may still persist. Priesthood, however, is still the principal social office of mediatorship between gods and humans, and as such is very important. The devouring aspect of the divine is considered to be very present and threatening, and the priesthood is as much engaged in deflecting divine wrath as it is in securing the gifts of and celebrating divine love. One is reminded in this context of the ancient Aztec civilization of Mexico, where the coming of solar eclipses and other unusual astronomical or natural phenomena were accompanied by human sacrifices. Analogous conditions existed in other civilizations. So in this phase of society the consciousness of the cosmos and of universal being is seen as a threatening power, not only as a benevolent one. This duality is really the recognition, one might say, at a projected level, of the ambivalence, the coexisting good and evil nature of the psyche. The universe, like the psyche, is not all good, not all bad, but both, and both qualities can come forth and manifest. Thus the unconscious must be supplicated and appeased to nourish and support us, and its destructive and devouring aspects must be kept from harming us. Such supplication is an important aspect of this phase of religiosity, for it is, of course, religion that addresses itself to societal protection.

Occasionally, of course, some advanced egos are born into this phase of society. They may try to challenge the vitally powerful, but at the same time dark and oppressive supremacy of the unconscious. But these individuals usually do not last, because they are out of harmony with the unconscious of the majority of the people. The unconscious devours them, a pattern which persists for a very long time. Historically, we find that all cultures go through a similar phase, and that even today, many cultures are still heavily involved in this phenomenon. Time and again, the collective lack of consciousness devours the heroic consciousness that rises to challenge it. Socrates drank hemlock because his was an ego that had outgrown the collective, and therefore the political leaders, exponents of the collectivity, came to him and said: "You, Socrates, are teaching doctrines which amount to the corruption, the moral corruption of the young of Athens." These leaders had no television or other modern media with which to attack Socrates, as they would today, but they were quite effective in carrying out their purposes, nevertheless.

In contrast to Socrates, the Hebrew prophets (with some exceptions, of course) appear to have been agents of the great unconscious tyranny embodied in their God. The barely emancipated, rebellious egos of various kings, cities and people were beaten into submission to the Jehovic archetype by the exhortations of its prophetic agents. It is difficult and often impossible for a heroic individual consciousness to succeed against the unconscious collectivity, especially in the developmental phase of culture we are describing. For example, the medieval emperors who rose against the Popes never really succeeded. Why? Because the Pope spoke for the unconscious collectivity, and the people were under the sway of the unconscious. The Hohenstauffen emperors, especially the cultured and enlightened Frederick II, tried to combat the power of the Papacy and of the Church, but they eventually ended up doing what came to be known as "going to Canossa" to kiss the foot of the Pope again.

In this manner the rebellious ego tries to rise against the unconscious, but cannot succeed; it then goes back, makes up and bows to the unconscious once more. How often one sees this in one's childhood and early adolescence. How dearly we all would have liked to tell our parents to go to the deepest Dantean circle of hell, so that we could be sovereign and autonomous, but at this stage of development, we were still lacking in power, and thus we could not do it. So perhaps we told them off with great drama and bluster and kicked up a good fuss —perhaps even ran away—but in the end, we came back and made up. After all, we still needed our meals; we still needed a bed to sleep in; and so we crawled back into the restrictive, but still protective nest.

The political analogies to this phase of development in many parts of the world are just as dramatic. Look at the recent and current situation in Iran. This archaic, backward country was taken over after World War I by a military officer who became Shah Reza I of the house of Pahlevi. He tried, like a good, heroic ego, to do away with at least the worst manifestations of the dark unconscious. He tried to secularize the country by taking away the power of the Mullahs and establishing a government independent of the domination of archaic, unconscious, religious structures. His son, Shah Mo-

hammed Reza, continued the task of civilizing, ur-
banizing and educating. Yet the backlash of the dark,
chthonic archetypes of the unconscious could not be
avoided. Out of his repressed exile in France came the
black-clad, black-turbaned, black-souled Ayatollah
Khomeni, like an avenging angel of the unconscious, a
dark archetype risen from the pit. We all know what
happened. The dark unconscious took over and established Mullah rule, theocracy; it turned Iranian history
back to the dark middle ages. In other places, notably in
Turkey, a similar development occurred, but without
an effective backlash. Mustafa Kemal Atatürk, affec-
tionately called Kemal the drunkard for his alcoholic
defiance of the law of the Prophet, took over and
secularized the country. He outlawed the fez worn by
men and tore the veil off the women. He told the clergy
to be quiet and to keep quiet, or else! Turkey is still not a
paragon of modern civilization and culture, but it is not
a theocratic dictatorship like Iran.

In many countries, this phase of the great unconscious mother—Mother Unconscious—still predomi-
nates and keeps the freedom of the ego at a nonexistent
or at least minimal level. Examples are numerous. Not
only the Islamic countries, but interestingly and para-
doxically enough, the Marxist countries, where the materialistic religion known as Marxism-Leninism has
taken over the role of the Church, illustrate this phase.
Many people don't recognize this fact. Religion, particularly unconscious, chthonic, archaic, old-time
religion comes in many guises. Even an atheistic religion like Communism is still a religion in the sense that
it takes over and demands total allegiance from individuals, just like the unconscious does. The Marxist-
Leninist religion has its rituals, dogmas and commandments. The party is the Church; its functionaries are the

clergy. What the medieval church was in Europe, the Communist party was in the Soviet Union and the Eastern bloc countries and remains so in countries such as Vietnam, Cuba and China. The party chairman is the Pope; he is the superior of presidents, premiers and the like, just as the Pope was the supreme overseer of emperors, kings and princes. And, of course, such countries have a most efficient inquisition. During the last world war, I had the opportunity of observing the political commissars of the Red Army in action. It was an awesome experience. One could see staff officers of the rank of colonel shiver in their boots before the commissars and their political police. One may imagine similar scenes during the era of the Inquisition, when knights and generals trembled before the cruel Dominican monks. Look around the world, and observe where there is the least personal freedom. You will certainly single out the Islamic theocracies and the Communist states. Why? Because they are both dominated by religion; in one case a theocratic ideology that has not progressed since the sixth century, and in the other, by an atheistic religion, following the prophets Marx and Lenin, or for that matter, Mao. All of these ideological tyrannies are in reality representatives of Great Mother Unconscious. Interestingly enough, these countries are always welfare states as well as tyrannies.

The tyrannical welfare state is, in fact, the best symbol of Great Mother Unconscious. "If you are a good kid, I will take care of you," says the Great Mother embodied in the state. "I will feed you; I will house you; I will give you work. If you don't tow the line, I will punish you, even devour you. I will put you into a concentration camp, into the Gulag. I will sacrifice you, because after all, you are my child, and that means that you are part of me. You cannot ever be an individual apart from me." Thus speaks the Great Mother Unconscious in her form as the tyrannical welfare state. In speaking so, she sounds just like a real undeveloped, unconscious mother, of whom there are many. Such mothers never want to grant their children sovereignty or real individuality, but continue instead to regard their children as extensions of themselves, even when they are old and gray. In the same manner, the totalitarian state always suppresses the individuality of its children. The motto of the totalitarian state is, "I am mother, and mother knows best." To this you may add, "And mother will get you if you are not good as she decrees!"

By painting this picture of the unconscious I don't mean to imply that this vital portion of the psyche is exclusively, or even primarily negative in its relationship to the conscious ego. Assuredly, the unconscious is the source of creativity, inspiration and psychic energy. Because of this, the ego is in great need of adequate avenues of access to the unconscious. By the same token we need to be aware that our unconscious selfhood, including the collective unconscious or objective psyche, is characterized by ambivalence toward the conscious ego. Mother Unconscious, as we called it, is devouring as well as nourishing, obscuring as well as illuminating, because it contains all polarities and can manifest them as it chooses. The tyrannical welfare state as a metaphor for a particular aspect of the unconscious needs to be understood within such a wider context.

The Patriarchal Period

The third phase of the growth and development of the individual psyche and of culture is what Erich Neumann refers to as the patriarchal period, or the phase of the Great Father or the spiritual father. In the psychic life of the individual, this phase concerns the rising of the power of the ego, and the consequent ascendancy of the conscious ego over its opposite number, the unconscious. At this point, the unconscious is increasingly rejected and depreciated. The rational ego creates its own goals and disciplines, which inevitably strive for personal independence, will and sovereignty. The political implications of this phase, I think, are most interesting, because they have a deep and direct bearing upon our own civilization, culture and systems of government.

Now, we must remember that in the main, religion is the representative of the greater unconscious background in every culture. Thus it is understandable that the first element, or force, with which the newly sovereign ego is likely to clash is religion, in whatever form it may exist in a particular society. In order to emancipate itself from the thralldom of the unconscious and its archetypes, the ego establishes, works for or tries to establish a secular political structure which is emancipated from the establishments of religion. The kings of the absolutist era refused to bow to the Pope and ruled their kingdoms without deferring to ecclesiastical power. The preference of absolutist monarchs for Protestantism as a form of religion, as manifest in Germany and in England, can be traced back to this psycho-historical element. Some reliance on religious symbols and moral precepts remained, but the crucial difference was that the state was regarded as a legitimate power in its own right which did not have to rely on the grace and approval of the religious power. In this phase, the state no longer derives its authority and justification from a supernatural, transcendental, religious mythos of some kind. The Renaissance period in Europe, and subsequently the Reformation, which freed secular rulers from ecclesiastical domination and control, were the real beginnings of this development in Western society. These developments were succeeded by the era of the Enlightenment and, finally, by the turbulent era of the French Revolution, during which the idea of popular sovereignty and individualism was advocated, although perhaps not implemented all that successfully.

This brings us to the situation in the United States. The American colonies, which separated themselves from the British mother country, were the offspring par excellence of the era of the Enlightenment. The U.S. Constitution asserted the disestablishment of religion, or as it is popularly described, the separation of church and state. The state vowed to be and to remain free and above religious disputes and principles, while allowing complete freedom of religion to its citizens. These principles led in America to a flowering of religious movements and sects perhaps unprecedented in history. The dire predictions of older religious establishments, such as the Roman Catholic Church, to the effect that a secular state would lead to the death of religion and to moral degradation were not fulfilled. On the contrary, America became a very religious country, in which religion flourished, but in a new way. The new way of religion in America was an individual way, a way of highly pluralistic personal religiosity.

We may say that religious life in America came to combine the highly individualistic attitudes of the ego with the search for the values of the unconscious as represented by religion itself. The devouring, repressive aspects of Mother Unconscious manifesting as Mother Church were greatly mitigated against by the state, which guaranteed the possibility of religious freedom and, to the best of its ability, guarded this freedom for its citizens. Probably not since Hellenistic Rome and Alexandria has there been such a combination of individualism and religion as has been seen throughout the history of the United States. For fifteen hundred years or more, such a phenomenon was not seen in Western society. While religious plurality no doubt has its shortcomings, its advantages were and are, I think, enormous. In fact, they are so great that they cannot be exaggerated.

The Integrative Phase

The essentially individualistic and libertarian religious life of the people of the United States has an important potential relationship to the fourth phase of the growth and development of the psyche, which Erich Neumann called the integrative phase. Neumann's theory declares that the father-oriented, ego-dominated patriarchal phase leaves the individual one-sided and incomplete. Important psychic elements, which may have feminine overtones, have been repressed and neglected. Consciousness and ego have been overvalued, and the non-rational, unconscious side of life has been depreciated. Individuality and personality have been exalted at the expense of the feeling-toned values of relatedness, emotion and community. Having wandered far and long from the unconscious homeland, the ego in this phase feels like a motherless child. So another change or transition to an integrative phase is needed to redeem these neglected psychic elements.

How does this transition manifest at the political level? Beginning in the 1930s or 40s, the public philosophy of the United States increasingly began to move away from the individualism of the era of the Enlightenment and of the Industrial Revolution. We may regard this movement away from rugged individualism as an indication of the beginnings of the integrative phase in the psycho-history of this country. At the same time, one is bound to admit that these stirrings of the integrative phase remained, in the main, rather confusing and confused. While an increasing number of cultured and well-meaning persons were beginning to see the need to recover the neglected psychic elements of the culture, the ways in which they went about this task produced many counterproductive results. The growth of the welfare state brought with it the rise of an inefficient and soulless bureaucracy and a clumsy and exceedingly costly apparatus of administrative governmental organs, which became a veritable millstone around the neck of American society. Many people became childishly dependent on the ministrations of the welfare state and regressed into mass-mindedness and unconsciousness. The educational methods and system broke down, bringing widespread custodial care of young persons, to whom not even the most essential elements of education were offered. The educational process became largely a mockery and a sham. The fanciest and most expensive public school systems in the world turned out vast numbers of functional illiterates and still continue to do so.

Once again, the analogy between the psychological development of the individual and the culture holds true. When the pressure within the field of the ego mounts toward the need to integrate unconscious content, the possibility always exists that this unconscious content will not be consciously integrated, but will instead overpower the ego and cause a psychic regression. Thus the impulse to move forward causes a step backward, as it were. Instead of becoming more conscious, the person becomes increasingly unconscious. Similarly, when the neglected side of society is given a chance to come forward, it can easily happen that things get out of hand, and that various regressive and chaotic conditions prevail.

From this it appears that the integrative phase of the psycho-historical growth of the culture of the United States has proceeded very laboriously. At the same time we must recognize, I think, that this phase, if it has indeed arrived at all, is of very recent origin. Therefore, to view these developments in the perspective of a mere fifty years is a mistake. It has taken hundreds, indeed thousands of years for civilizations to go through these phases, or to pass from one to another. What is needed at the present time is a very philosophical, serene and detached view of these developments. Instead of allowing ourselves to be thrown into a frenzy of excitement because of the conditions existing around us, we have to see that the social, political and historical process occurs in time, and since it is a process within time, it takes time. It would be as realistic to imagine that from one year to the next a New Age has burst upon the world, in which all things have rapidly changed to a paradisical condition, as it would be to regard the growing pains and confusions of the present era as indicating a frightful decadence and decline of the moral, intellectual, political and economic character of the culture.

Time and timelessness are one of the great pairs of opposites of our psyches. The ego functions in time; the unconscious exists outside of it. Thus we tend to look out into the world from the watchtower of our own archetypes, our own unconscious, and expect that this outer world will be able to conform in some fashion to the expectations of this interior, deeply unconscious vision. In the unconscious, things can happen without the intervention of time and the impositions of space. The individual who is motivated by the archetypal realities of the unconscious can be heard to exclaim, "There is no reason whatsoever why we couldn't make a perfect society right now!" Of course there is no reason why one couldn't make a perfect society in one's head, in one's mind right now, but there are plenty of good reasons why one cannot create such a condition in the outer world. There is time to contend with, and there are a multitude of circumstances and forces working against one and against each other. A fiat arising out of the mind cannot change the world in the twinkling of an eye. Idealistic persons tend to expect their projections to assume a physical reality in the outer world very rapidly and without difficulty. This, of course, does not happen. Thus the impatient idealist is always disappointed and dejected.

One of the great stumbling blocks in the path of the growth and development of our culture within the context of an integrative phase of development has been our excessive extraversion of consciousness. When speaking of extraversion and introversion among peoples, Jung graphically and forcefully stated that "America is extraverted like hell." Thus, the prevailing attitude of this country makes it understandable that extraverted, and consequently, simple-minded and reductionistic approaches should prevail here when it comes to creative social and economic change. Just think of it. A supposedly religious, idealistic nation, which is ever proclaiming its ideals and spiritual commitments, at the same time always gives priority to economic and material considerations when it comes to social development. Isn't this quite the same thing that the Marxists do, when they look upon history as being determined exclusively by economic forces? Thus we have reformers, the potential agents of the incipient in-

tegrative phase of psycho-history, addressing themselves first and foremost to the economic structure of the
culture. By attacking and undermining the nineteenth
century model of free market economy, or what was
classically called economic liberalism, these reformers
start at the very worst place. By attacking the freedom
of the market place they have almost succeeded in killing the goose that laid the golden egg of America's economic power and prosperity. The result is confusion,
the diminishing of economic resources within the individual sphere and the collectivistic growth of the
welfare state—not a development conducive to an enhancement of consciousness and individuation to be
sure! What has happened, of course, is that the
economic cart was tackled before the psychological
horse; the spiritually natural order of priorities was
reversed because of the extraverted and implicitly materialistic attitude of consciousness prevailing in the
minds of the leaders and thinkers of society.

What we have neglected is the psychological fact that
useful advances in culture must begin at the level of the
mind, rather than at the level of physical conditions.
Jung put it very well when he said: "Every advance in
culture is psychologically an extension of consciousness,
a coming to consciousness that can take place only
through discrimination. Therefore an advance always
begins with individuation, that is to say, with the individual, conscious of his isolation cutting a new path
through hitherto untrodden territory."

We are then currently in America dealing with a pioneering effort of consciousness, cutting through previously untrodden territory, which to a large extent must
occur at the individual level and primarily psychologically. The thrust of this movement toward growth
must be psychological rather than economic or politi-

cal. In this respect both the left and the right, the liberal
and the conservative positions, are in serious need
of rethinking their premises and methods; they must
abandon their materialism and excessive extraversion
and acquire a psychological sense, which they so woefully lack. Changes, if they are to be creative, lasting
and consistent with the psycho-historical needs of the
culture, must start in consciousness.

Motivations for Social Transformation

The only recent development that creatively combined
social and psychological change may have been the up-
surgence of new consciousness in the 1960s and 1970s,
when a counter- or underground culture of unprecedented magnitude grew up within the majority culture. In spite of its many shortcomings, the counterculture brought to the fore tremendously transformative and liberating forces of far-reaching dimensions. It
is easy, and frequently done, to reduce the developments of the 1960s and 1970s to such factors as drug use,
rock music, communal living situations, unusual and
distinctive forms of dress and the flaunting of previously
sacrosanct sexual morés. But, I think, these superficiali-
ties had very little to do with what really happened at
this curiously transformative period of our history.

Robert Evans in *Belief and Counterculture* defined
the motivations which played the greatest role within
and behind the developments of the 60s and 70s as
follows: (1) priority of experience and subjective involvement in experience; (2) recovery of mystery and
restoration of creativity; (3) concern for communication and the symbolic dimension; and (4) revitalization
of community and openness to transcendence.

In the following, we shall look very briefly at some of

these motivations to see how valuable they might be and why there has been such a tremendous reaction against them on the part of religious crusaders who feel threatened by the changes in consciousness in our culture. Let us begin with what Evans termed "the priority of experience." What is experience? True experience is a rare bird in our world, and particularly in our culture as it has developed. Why is this so? Because our culture, from a certain time on, became geared to what might be called substitutional experience rather than to direct experience. Technology is one factor involved in this shift, but the real culprit is a state of mind characterized by an exaltation of the thinking function. Some people, who are opposed to the trend of substitutional experience in our culture, have become enraged at technology. This reaction is definitely misguided. Technology itself is not behind all that has gone wrong in America. Technology cannot really do anything to us, unless large psychological factors are also involved. No doubt technology supplied us with the tools of substitutionalism, but it did not supply the motive, for that was psychological. The motives behind the rise of substitutional experience were supplied by very old and dark unconscious patterns of the mind, which predate technology by millenia. Without a doubt, the Semitic God-concept of old Jehovah had much to do with it. From this worldview we learned that substitutional experience is moral and permissible, while direct experience is either immoral, or, at least, dangerously bordering on immorality.

As the result of psychological developments of long standing, the substitutional experience has become the normative experience. Truth has become abstract and theoretical, in lieu of what it should be: namely, concrete and existential. Modern psychological research, especially that of Jung, has brought back to us the emphasis we need on the importance of psychology over abstract meaning, and consequently on existential over theoretical truth. Through depth psychology we are beginning to find that there is really no truth "out there" in the region of abstractions, but only truth within ourselves. In a sense, it might be said that there is no "truth" as such, but only "my truth" as it occurs within the existential and phenomenological reality of my own interior being. The "truth" derived from substitutional experience is, of course, diametrically opposed to such valid psychological recognitions.

Michael Novak in *The Experience of Nothingness* has said, "The accusations of the counterculture are not attacks upon intelligent, accurate understanding or good judgment, but upon the myth of objectivity as too narrow an expression of reason which leaves out of consideration too many delicate but crucial operations of human intelligence." The "myth of objectivity" is, of course, intimately connected with the issue of substitutional experience. Long before the contemporary counterculture, Carl Jung exploded the myth of objectivity on the basis of depth psychology. He said, in effect, that what most people conceive of as objective is, in reality, the most subjective thing in the world. Why? Because it is chock-full of the projections of the observer! Most people, because of their relative lack of integrated consciousness, are well-nigh incapable of anything resembling objective observations and judgments. Only a highly individuated person, who has accomplished a great measure of the integration of the conscious and unconscious elements in his or her psyche, is capable of true objectivity. Until that point is reached, we inevitably find a great deal of unassimilated unconscious content projecting itself into our field of vision. We think that we are being objective, but in reality, we are mistaking our projections for objective reality.

Our quest for true objectivity is thus another manifestation of the striving for direct experience. However, we must remember in this context that many people in society are threatened by the possibility of direct experience and of true, psychological objectivity. There are always people about who have vested interests in the normative character of substitutional experience, people who in some way derive profit from the fact that direct experience is not available or not considered right. These people, ranging from television preachers to police commissioners, are committed to denying people the freedom to create and experience their own reality. When we are able to experiment with alternative modalities of feeling and of behavior, then these and similar merchants of the existing established models will begin to lose out.

The second important element which the counterculture has brought forth is what Evans calls "the recovery of mystery and creativity." What really happened is that people discovered once again that to address themselves to the mysterious and to the creative recesses of the unconscious is a vital and real task; that without mystery and creativity, life is not worthwhile. Here too, the advocates of old-time religion feel threatened. For many centuries they have attempted to exorcise the elements of mystery and creativity from the life of our culture. To them, creativity is a sacrilegious attempt to duplicate the creation ability of their God. There has been one creation already, and that is quite enough, or so they think. And what mysteries does the human being need that are not covered by the Bible? Human beings are supposed to be creatures and not creators in the eyes of such folk, and mysteries are simply not needed, thank you! The perennial Gnostic striving for mystery and for creativity is thus anathema indeed to all advocates of old-time unconscious religiosity.

The third motivation mentioned by Evans is "concern for communication and the symbolic dimension." With the recovery of the symbolic dimension comes what one may call the transvaluation of symbols. Unconscious religiosity of the old-time variety has its own symbols and makes the most of them for its own benefit. The unconscious of humanity is ruled by symbols, but when symbols are not consciously understood, they become tyrants and idols in one's life. For example, the issues of abortion and birth control are assuredly symbolic, which is why unconscious old-time religion harps on them with such persistence and vehemence. What is the symbol behind these issues? It is the archetype of the Great Devouring Mother, an unconscious archetype of nature and of natural law. The dynamism of the Great Mother wants to give birth, no matter what the conditions or what the birth might do to the psychological or material welfare of the potential parents. The Mother will not be thwarted or interfered with. It is important to note that the emotionalism and blind unconsciousness of some extreme devotees of the ecology and nature movement are similar in their effect to religious unconsciousness. Ecological extremism and right-to-life fanaticism are brothers underneath their unconscious skins. Both may reflect unconscious worship of what appears to them the supreme value: life. But some may forget that life without consciousness is a blind, brutal surge, a force without direction or purpose, a torrent of energy coming from no place and going nowhere.

Thus the devouring and birthgiving Mother as a huge, unconscious archetype looms over the symbolic issues of birth control and abortion. From this awesome symbol of the collective unconscious, issues relating to human reproduction derive their power and relevance. And hasn't the Church been called since early times *Mater Ecclesia*, Mother Church? Placating a powerful archetype is the problem at the unconscious level, which, being unconscious, is, of course, not recognized.

When individuating, conscious persons begin to strive for their own symbolic reality, they run up against the tyrannical influence of the great unconscious symbols which have been enshrined by various religious establishments, whose adherents have simply worshipped what they did not understand. Today, many persons are seeking once more for the symbols of transformation which arise from a deeper level of personal experience. For such symbols to be transformative, they have to be realized at an individual and personal level. That is why so many individuals were and are not satisfied with the established symbol systems of our culture, but seek the amplification of their symbolic quest in various nonestablishment symbols, such as Tarot cards, astrological signs, magical sigils, mandalas and the like. All of this activity is, of course, anathema to those who feel that the "old rugged cross" is all one can possibly need as a meaningful symbol of life.

The fourth motivation mentioned by Evans is the "revitalization of community" and the "openness to transcendence" within a community. Communitarianism, we must remember, is by no means the same as communism. The commune or community need not be an expression of collective mass-mindedness, although it often becomes just that. Individuals must be able to make decisions as to what kind of community or communalism they wish to be part of. They must not be forced into a community by external pressures, by the secret police and the commissar, as it were, but freely choose or create communal situations on the basis of their personal predilections and interests. Thus the communist system says to people: I am your community and you had better accept this community, or else! In a somewhat similar manner, old-time unconscious religion says: We have a society that is pleasing unto God as it is, and you had better accept it as it is, and behave within it, or else. The great difference is, however, that in our society, with its constitutional freedoms, an individual is at least legally free to tell the old-time preachers and their kith and kin to go to Hades, and to go about choosing his or her own communal associations on the basis of personal preference, compatibility and so forth.

At this point in time the countercultural trends of the 60s and the 70s, along with other developments, have produced what might be called a revolt against the old symbolic structures and community ideals by emerging pluralistic models of community, which are based on freely chosen personal relatedness and the relationship of sovereign individuals. These new communities are supplanting the much more unconscious archetypal community bonding based on ties of blood and nation. The frantic cries about "saving the family," as well as the mindless superpatriotism evident among religious crusaders, can be explained as a reaction against this trend. Certainly no one would claim that there is no place in society for family, but by the same token, one must recognize that there are valid forms of association which are based on conscious considerations rather than on unconscious and choiceless belonging to a group. If consciousness is worth more than unconsciousness, and if choice is preferable to lack of choice, then there must be a possibility of communities freely entered into, which may supersede and even replace the natural, but thereby unconscious, unit of the family. A family is a fine thing, to be sure, but conscious persons may find values that are superior to those of the family. Similarly, an intelligent, conscious patriotism is a commendable position, but with the growth of consciousness, it is quite likely that supranational values and loyalties may also make themselves felt in the psyche of the individual.

Combatting the Threats to Freedom

To summarize our psycho-historical analysis of the present assault on the changes in consciousness and morality, we note once again that these changes are conceived by some religious crusaders as heralding the ultimate moral degradation and downfall of America. Their efforts represent a resistance of unconscious, archaic forces against the growing trends toward individuation and the growth of consciousness in our age. The Moloch of mass-mindedness once again appears to be demanding a sacrifice of our personal selfhood and our right to individual choices. Today and any day, it is incumbent on those who cherish personal freedom and the opportunities for free spiritual growth to realize that threats to freedom are to be taken seriously, whether they come from the quarters of Marxism or from those of a home-grown politicized religiosity. The tyranny of Marxist collectivism and the would-be religious control of the moral climate and personal lives of the citizens of our country are both cut from the same psychological cloth. Both are expressions of the primitive unconscious. The Lords of the Kremlin, the bloodthirsty fanatics of Cambodia, the religious butchers of Iran and the self-righteous politicized television preachers of our country are instruments of the same psychological forces. They are anti-individuational and collectivist in their thrust—primitive soul-killing forces, bent upon establishing and preserving their own power, which is rooted in the dark impulses and subrational needs of the unconscious.

What is the relationship of these anti-individual forces to conservatism? Observed from a historical perspective, these movements are the antithesis of real conservatism. In my view, true conservatism is always libertarian rather than authoritarian in its emphasis. Modern conservative philosophy originated with the English philosopher Edmund Burke, who, repelled by the excesses of the French Revolution, established a spiritual orientation rooted in conserving the values of the past, combined with a profound respect for the dignity and freedom of the individual. Burke's conservatism was thus a libertarian conservatism, which opposed the reign of terror in France and similar phenomena on the basis of a regard for individual liberty against collective terror and tyranny. We need to recognize in this context, of course, that conservatism and progressivism are neither more nor less than expressions of the eternally present principle of pairs of opposites in the world. When we become exceedingly attached to one member of a pair to the exclusion of the other, we create a dangerous imbalance.

Moreover, the conditions, values and situations of the past need to be conserved. Out of the old comes the new. If we want to hatch chickens, we must preserve the eggs and not break and devour them before the chickens have a chance to hatch. Revolutionaries all too often break the eggs of the past, and thus find themselves without a creative and promising future. All too often, they use up their historical credit by doing away with the elements of the past; then they are left with nothing, except perhaps some cultural eggshells. On the other hand, it is obvious that things are not wonderful and worthy of eternal life just because they are old. Old things can be quite useless, although not necessarily so. Thus for real change to take place, we must adopt neither an unconscious conservatism that hangs onto anything that is old for dear life, nor a mindless, compulsive progressivism that pursues change for the sheer joy of change. What America needs are individuals who are capable of balanced, conscious choices, freely arrived at and peacefully and freely implemented within the framework of a flexible, libertarian society. In contrast, the design, intentions and more particularly the methods of the politicized religionists in our midst are characterized by at best a pseudo-conservatism. It should be apparent to all insightful and philosophical conservatives of the Burkeian variety that it is unbecoming to their position and stature to be bedfellows of the vulgar primitivism and the potential collective tyranny of those who mindlessly serve the archaic unconscious archetypes of past ages, and who are willing to sacrifice to these archetypes the greatest value to be conserved in our society: namely, freedom.

One more point needs to be raised here, the issue of morality, under the banner of which so much nonsense is propagandized today. A conscious psychological attitude toward ethical issues always distinguishes between two kinds of morality: individual and public. Religions the world over can address themselves with some degree of legitimacy to individual morality. Based on their particular metaphysical models of reality, various religions can establish guidelines and, occasionally, quite rigid commandments regarding the ways individuals ought to behave in order to live in harmony with a particular metaphysical reality. Religious authorities have always felt that the regulation or at least the influencing of the moral behavior of individual believers was within their province. As long as these ethical maxims are accepted more or less freely by individuals within a particular religious context, this is really no more than the proper exercise of personal freedom and choice. The difficulty arises, however, when religious believers, and their leaders, who fail to distinguish between private and public morality, assume that what they consider to be the right standards of behavior for themselves ought to be the right standards for all persons in the community or the society at large.

What happens when religious morality, intended for the use of the individual, is foisted on the entire body politic? The result is that the growth and development of consciousness in such a society is greatly restricted. Consciousness grows not by right behavior, but by behavior that is the result of free, conscious decisions and choices. Real morality involves freedom. This is the mystery of the Christian teaching of free will, so egregiously abused and misunderstood by many Christians themselves. Free will is a valuable psychological teaching when properly understood. According to this teaching, God has not exercised the prerogative of forcing human beings onto a path of virtue, but instead gave humans the supreme opportunity of choice. Free will is an accepted doctrine of the Christian faith. However, these implications are often ignored by the self-appointed guardians of Christian morality, who forever try to improve on the method adopted by their deity by attempting to force their private morality and commandments upon society by way of legislation, law enforcement and other forms of coercion. Isn't it curious that while God gave humanity a choice, God's devout servants are busily trying to take that same choice away? Somewhere within the tangled structures of theology and Biblical exegesis is concealed a forgotten, but all-important truth: that God offered humans a choice because God desired them to grow and not merely to remain fixed in one condition, even if that condition is obedience to God's law. Ironically, God did not force people to obey divine laws, but God's servants attempt to do just that.

The chief characteristic of increasing individuation within society is choice, which includes the exercise of free will. Morality in such an instance is increasingly a private concern, and public laws and regulations are restricted to a sphere in which they are motivated by the realistic welfare of the community and not by abstract and theoretical considerations of right and wrong. Every religious organization has its moral and ethical doctrines. Dogma, morals and ritual are the inevitable trinity of any religious system. It would be foolish to demand or even to wish that churches and synagogues not teach some form of morality. What needs to be kept in mind, however, is that a religious group can claim the right to impose its regulations and laws only upon its own members, who abide by them by their own free choice. When the moral strictures and religious laws of a particular sect are elevated to the status of secular law and are enforced on all citizens of whatever belief or none, then we are unquestionably in the grip of a tyranny.

Libertarian and freethinking individuals frequently make the mistake of wishing to dictate to various groups and individuals ways in which they should accord more freedom to their believers and followers. However, as long as a group's followers obey the dictates of their superiors as the result of their own free choice, they must be accorded the privilege of obedience or "unfreedom," even as others must be given the choice of freedom. No one can presume to tell the Pope to approve of abortion or birth control or any other policy. After all, if someone does not like the policies of the Pope, he or she can easily leave the Roman Catholic Church and find a more congenial religious conviction. If the Hari Krishna movement, Rajneesh or another spiritual leader imposes curious regulations on his or her followers, that is their own business. But when religious folk move surreptitiously or—as now is often the case, brazenly—into the process of legislation, into government or the courts, and demand that their particular and private morality be made public law, binding for all, then they must be told in no uncertain terms that they are wrong. If that is not enough, they ought to be prevented by all lawful means from carrying out their ill-advised designs.

Finally, I think it is high time that matters of social morality and behavior be viewed in a historical and even a psycho-historical perspective. It is easy to become excessively concerned over some real or imagined evil in society and furiously demand regulations and changes to address this condition. When separated from their larger, historical context, many conditions appear momentous and disastrous. Thus people can get exercised over what seems to be the erosion of the moral fiber of the nation or the deterioration of the moral standards of the culture. A lack of a historical perspective always brings with it a lack of proportion. Issues tend to become inflated and distorted; mountains and molehills are confused; minor matters appear bigger than life. Out of such conditions come intemperate policies, unwise decisions, hasty and oppressive legislation and, in their wake, social conditions which take many years to remedy and which make for the oppression of unborn generations. All of this comes about because people have no sense of history, no way of evaluating their present concerns and perplexities in the light of the past.

The historical roots of our present politico-religious concerns are readily discernible to the informed eye. The founders of the American republic were men of the era of the Enlightenment, who were zealously guarding the new-found freedoms of the individual soul and mind from the renewed encroachments of archaic unconscious forces. As previously stated, the separation of church and state was a great historical landmark guaranteeing the emancipation of the human ego from the tyranny of the unconscious archetypes. Enlightenment means the coming of the light of the conscious ego and the receding of the collective, murky unconsciousness. Franklin, Washington, Jefferson, the enlightened Freemasons and spiritual libertarians wished to bring about a social setting in which free minds and souls could grow and individuate according to the laws of their inner being, without domination by psychological structures carried over from the Middle Ages, which had outlived their usefulness.

Today, the descendants of these enlightened founders have, for the most part, lost their psychological connection with the intentions of these wise men, who despite their powdered wigs and lace cuffs, were mapping out a plan of individuation, spiritual growth and freedom unprecedented in the recorded history of our world. We have allowed the myopia of the present to rob us of the consciousness of our past, and thus we are in great danger of forfeiting our future. The keynote of this noble experiment of the enlightenment that became the United States of America was and is not morality or Judeo-Christian rectitude, although these were, of course, part of the heritage of the American people, but rather it was always *choice*. Choice has made thousands of religions and philosophies flourish side by side on American soil. Choice brought free public education to all the children of the people. Choice produced an economy that facilitated a standard of living unknown anywhere on the globe in any era of history. The opportunity of choice has been the great and, in many ways, the unique gift of the gods to the people of this land. This is not to say that there were and are not great imperfections and inequities commingling with the element of choice. One was slavery, with its still present results. Another was the ill treatment of the native population of the land. Social and historical ills and evils have existed and persist here in abundance. Still, the glorious element of choice has always worked its way forward and onward through the darkness and the evils. I like to nourish the hope that choice, or I might say freedom, is still with us and is still moving forward on the pathway of history.

Western culture is the only culture in history that has taken time seriously, and thus has managed to achieve consciousness and autonomy from the vast, unconscious dragon and its tyranny. It is true that this autonomy has been costly, and that now, in the dawning integrative phase of psycho-history, we must placate and understand the dragon once again. In time, and within the context of a consciously realized history, we must make our peace with the dragon. As individual, individuated heroes of consciousness we must descend into the underworld, into the caverns where the dragons dwell. Carrying the torch of consciousness, we must illuminate the murky labyrinths of the psyche and bring forth the treasures guarded by the great worms of the mind. For the first time in many thousands of years we have the tools and the equipment to do this, and on a fairly large scale. Tools of information and education are available to us which previous generations and civilizations lacked. But to do this work, we must be free. We must not be deprived of the great treasure bequeathed to us by the wise men of old; we must continue to possess choice. Without choice, our heroic quest shall be in vain. Without choice, the torch of our consciousness will lose its illuminating flame. Without choice, our history will have occurred in vain, our struggles and battles will have been to no purpose.

Today, as ever, there are those who would deprive us of our opportunity of choice. Some of these enemies of choice are wrapped in the red banner of Marxism and others (incredibly) wrap themselves in the star-spangled banner itself. Some would rob us of the choice of consciousness in the name of dialectical materialism, while others would do so in the name of the Bible. The curious irony of all this is that many of these people are filled with good intentions. Some wish to erase poverty, and others to do away with crime and vice. In their own fashion, they, too, strive for the good. Still, I say, they must be resisted strenuously, vigilantly and mightily. We cannot compromise with those who would take away from us the prize of choice. We may not have a just society or a virtuous society, but we can have, we must have, a society where choice is possible. We may not be wealthy, or healthy or righteous, but we can be free. We may not have the guarantee of ease, or of happiness, or of salvation, but we have the opportunity of growth. And for this we must continue to strive, and this we must defend!

3

Anima and Animus in Society:
Should the Sexes Ever Be Equal?

Historical inquiry has always been greatly motivated by
a concern for the future. At first glance it might appear
as if history embodies a concern for and a preoccupation
with the past, but this is not entirely true. As long ago as
the days of ancient China, the great master-philosopher
Confucius declared that of the three dimensions of
time, the past, the present, and the future, the one we
should chiefly value is the past. Confucius said that the
present is always unclear; the future, not having occurred yet, is at best a matter of conjecture; thus the
past is the only dimension which is available for the
purposes of inquiry, learning and the acquisition of
wisdom. The past, while unchangeable, is knowable;
therefore, the true historian, who by definition must be
a philosopher rather than a mere recorder of facts,
would for the most part agree with Confucius. He said
that which is proved by time cannot be assailed; while
that which is disproven by time cannot be justified.
When dealing with the perplexities of human history,
we must decide what it is that endures and is proven by

time. We must ask, in what way can we make our own the enduring truths of history, and by applying them within the present, modify the future in a way that will benefit our welfare.

Modern depth psychology has much to say regarding these questions, because it can establish certain analogies between the character and development of the individual on the one hand, and the unfoldment of history on the other. The human being is a world in miniature, and like human society, like the larger world outside, it develops according to certain historical patterns. Civilizations, nations and peoples live and mature, grow old and die very much like individuals, and are in fact composed of individuals whose psychological condition is reflected in society on a magnified scale. With the advent of depth psychology, therefore, historical research and especially the field of the philosophy of history have been greatly enriched.

The representative schools of depth psychology may be roughly divided into two groups: those which are backward looking, or reductionist, and those which are forward looking, or progressive. The school of Freud and some others who are closely allied to his methods may be considered as primarily backward looking. This means that present conditions within the individual psyche are almost inevitably explained as originating in the past, particularly in early childhood and infancy. On the other hand, Jung and those following his lead feel that the present state of the psyche is not exclusively or even chiefly determined by its past. Jung believed that the psychological development of a person can be traced not only backward toward a cause in the past, but forward toward a goal in the future. A teleological destiny beckons to us from the future and draws us toward itself.

This future, says Jung, is a goal of integrated wholeness, totality and completeness. In a sense, Freud and Jung are like Confucius and Lao-tzu come back into the modern West from their ancient Chinese setting. Like Confucius, Freud asserts that the past, being knowable, is an individual's most important guide. Jung, like Lao-tzu, seems to be saying that while the details, the particulars of the future, may be unknown, the pattern of future development is not. As every living thing has a natural tendency to fill out its innate pattern, so the soul or psyche has a way, a pattern, a Tao of its own, which it strives to manifest. The acorn grows into an oak, not into a pine; a rose hip becomes a rose and not a carnation; and each human being has a destiny of growth and fulfillment, which is special as well as natural, individual as well as collective. We are the way we are because the Tao of our being, the great enduring mystery, is ever trying to fulfill itself in us and through us. Something tugs and pulls at our being ceaselessly, and this something is an archetype of wholeness, of the oneness that Jung called the Self, the central archetype which organizes and marshals all other archetypes toward the goal of unity.

While the reductionist Freud, rather like Confucius, looks upon history as the cause of present ills, the psychological Taoism of Jung looks toward the transhistorical patterns of universal nature and eternal being as the determining factors of the psyche. Freud says that the infant within the individual remains in conflict with the social responsibilities of the adult. In his socially and historically oriented works, such as *Civilization and Its Discontents*, Freud postulates that primitive humanity struggled with the tendencies of civilization, which forced repression of instinctual power, foregoing of rape, stealing, mayhem and impulsiveness in favor of the regulated patterns of behavior in civilized society. Jung does not deny this idea in its totality. He recognizes that everyone carries a child and a primitive human being within. It is also true that, particularly in young people, a measure of such reductive analysis can be helpful. When young people come to recognize that certain counterproductive attitudes in their lives are merely survivals of infantile behavior, they can detach themselves from these and thus be helped toward a more mature attitude. But for the majority of us, it is not particularly helpful to feel that we are inwardly babies, or prehistoric men and women.

Thus we find that in the subjective life of the individual are to be found not only the causes of the ills of society, but also the potential remedies for at least a large number of these ills. If our primitive selfhood is in conflict with civilization within the subpersonal regions of our selfhood, it is equally true that on the other end of the great polarity, within the transpersonal aspects of our being, resides the archetypal Self—the reconciler, the peacemaker, the wise counsellor, the compassionate judge who grants absolution and brings about the just and natural order, symbolized in religion as the Kingdom of God. This Self is the Messiah, the Avatar, the coming Buddha, the Second Coming of Christ, the One who makes all things new, the paradigm of the individuated ego.

Anima and Animus

This brings us to the all-important archetypes of anima and animus and their social and historical implications. When studying the creation myths of ancient peoples the world over, one is struck by the fact that almost without exception these myths hold that creation begins with a primordial wholeness, which divides itself into two halves. By virtue of their separation, these two half-realities are then able to come together in a state of primordial procreative union, which in the Latin alchemical terminology is called *coniunctio oppositorum* ("the conjunction of opposites"). By way of this union, everything that fills the many worlds is brought into being. Still, so the great myths tell us, the principles of Yin and Yang, heaven and earth, the sun and the moon, are present in every form of manifest creation, and each quality is incomplete without its opposite. Theirs is a cosmic yearning, a mysterious longing after union that thrills through the whole world—the great sigh of cosmic lovers desirous of uniting with each other. "To me, to me," whisper the pine trees and thunders the fire of the heavens, as it flashes down in impetuous passion to earth. The ebb and flow of the vast oceans sigh with every wave, "To me, to me." One may say that this is mere romanticism, a poetic projection in which we perceive in the forces of nature our own inmost needs. But such disagreements matter little, for the fact is, whether in us or outside of us, we are bound to recognize a transpersonal or archetypal need for a conjunction of opposites, a hermetic marriage, a reconciliation of cosmic polarities.

C. G. Jung gave voice to this most significant truth when he spoke of the anima, the feminine soul, and the animus, the masculine soul, as coexisting in every human being. In an oversimplified manner, one might say that every man has a woman within him, and that every woman has a man within her. In the course of developing our conscious adaptation through the process of ego formation, we each largely repress that side of our nature which does not conform to our biological characteristics. The woman in man recedes to the unconscious level, and the man in the woman also retires behind the screen of unconsciousness. However, it is important to keep in mind that repression is not the only, or even the chief cause of the presence of a contrasexual component in the unconscious of every person. It is particularly important to emphasize this, because with the advent of the feminist movement, much passionate rhetoric is being devoted to these matters and the true factors are increasingly obscured. According to Jung, the social structure with its predetermined roles does not itself determine what contrasexual factors in us ought to be repressed. Society, of course, is always there, demanding in various ways that we develop characteristics which are appropriate to our sex and that we renounce others which are not. However, these elements of social conditioning, which incidentally are subject to change, are not the only factors which determine the receding of the feminine component into the background of the male, and the corresponding fading into unconsciousness of the masculine subself in the female.

Jung says that in addition to social pressure there are two other important factors, one biological and one archetypal— or as he calls them in one place, one physical and one spiritual. In the makeup of every man there is a biological presupposition that there is beside himself another being in the world—namely, woman. As Jung says, "[Man's] system is tuned in to woman from the start, just as it is prepared for quite a definite world where there is water, light, air, salt, carbohydrates, etc." A woman's organic background also presupposes man, since the biological preconditioning of her psyche prepares her for his existence. Now, neither of these factors is conscious. Social pressure starts on the conscious level, but it results in repression, and thus ends in the unconscious. The biological predetermination, on the other hand, is unconscious to begin with and remains largely on the unconscious level.

But there is yet another factor to consider, probably the most important of the three—namely, the archetypal. An archetype is not a product of society; neither is it something that emanates from biology. Archetypes are sovereign forms of being which live a life of their own. They draw us with titanic force to themselves, and if our attempts to understand them, to bring them into more or less conscious awareness, are successful, they may lead us to wholeness, to totality and to authentic selfhood, a process which Jung called individuation:

> Archetypes resemble the beds of rivers: dried up because the water has deserted them, though it may return at any time. An archetype is something like an old watercourse along which the water of life flowed for a time, digging a deep channel for itself. The longer it flowed the deeper the channel, and the more likely it is that sooner or later the water will return.
>
> *Civilization in Transition*

> Archetypes were, and still are, psychic forces that demand to be taken seriously, and they have a strange way of making sure of their effect. Always they were the bringers of protection and salvation, and their violation has as its consequence the "perils of the soul" known to us from the psychology of primitives. Moreover, they are the infallible causes of neurotic and even psychotic disorders, behaving exactly like neglected or maltreated physical organs or organic functional systems.
>
> *The Archetypes and the Collective Unconscious*

What then are we talking about when we speak of anima and animus on the individual and the social level? The anima in man and the animus in woman are the organizing matrix or nucleus around which all the qualities constellate themselves, which an individual lacks on the conscious level, but which he or she may live unconsciously. The anima is the great unknown for men, as is the animus for women. Both sexes experience a longing for the unknown, but also a sense of awe, fear and in extreme cases, hostility. Jung himself defines the anima figure as follows:

> Every man carries within himself an eternal image of woman, not the image of this or that definite woman, but rather a definite feminine image. This image is fundamentally an unconscious, hereditary factor of primordial origin, and is engraven in the living system of man, a "type" ("archetype") of all the experiences with feminine beings in the age-long ancestry of man, a deposit, as it were, of all the impressions made by woman; in short, an inherited psychical system of adaptation. Even if there were no women, it would be possible at any time to deduce from this unconscious image how a woman must be constituted psychically. The same is true of the woman; that is, she also possesses an innate image of man.
>
> *The Development of Personality*

The anima then is the enchantress, the great unknown for man, and the animus, the hero who rescues woman from the state of disunity. Both of these are potential guides to the depths of the unconscious; they can be our initiators into the royal secrets of the inner life, the torchbearers of individuation. However, for these archetypes to fulfill such a constructive role, men and women must learn to relate to them within themselves in a constructive way.

This is the point where we are apparently facing great and grave difficulties today. In recent decades the social component of the anima-animus archetype has undergone radical changes which are still going on. There is a widespread questioning of and even revolt against the roles in society that traditionally pertained to men and women. Along with many needed legal and social reforms, we also see a vast confusion of attitudes and values, and a questioning of the usefulness, even the desirability of sexual identity. This confusion has grave potential psychological consequences. The following points may help us to orient ourselves in the present chaos of the sexes:

1) Sexual differences are not only skin deep. There are psychological as well as physical differences between men and women, which cannot be glossed over without serious injury to the psyche.

2) The psychological differences between men and women are rooted not only in social indoctrination, but in the fundamental task peculiar to the masculine psyche, which is internal union with the anima, and to the feminine psyche, which is union with the animus.

3) Since anima (the enchantress) is a figure markedly different from animus (the hero) they must be approached in different ways. Thus it follows that the paths of individuation for men and women should be at least to a certain degree different.

4) Although the task of uniting the opposites is internal to the individual, it relates significantly and powerfully to the way men and women achieve relationships with each other on the outer level.

5) In our revisions of social standards and roles for men and women we must be careful not to trivialize the character of this relationship. No aspect of life should be deromanticized or trivialized. The archetypes of transforming power fled from marriages of convenience and convention, but they are also apt to be absent from many "liberated" relationships, where magic and

romance are exorcised by animus-possessed, fiercely rational women, and by mousy men lacking in ego strength.

6) Since the object of life is the union of anima and animus, we must first relate the egos of men and women to each other and then attempt to relate man to woman positively through his anima, and woman to man positively by way of her animus.

7) The ego is basically superficial in all persons. It wants to remain the master; it does not want individuation. If an untrained, neurotic ego attempts to relate to the opposite sex on the level of anima and animus, it courts disaster.

8) This disaster takes the form of inflation of the ego by the contrasexual image. Men become nagging, moody, petty, gossip-mongering and stubborn, and women, demanding, supercontrolling and always positive of being right. Says Jung in the fifth of *The Seven Sermons to the Dead*, "Man and woman become a devil to each other when they do not separate their spiritual paths, for the nature of a created being is always differentiation."

9) All that is outside is really inside first. If a man is afraid of women, or hostile to women, or has a compulsive urge to dominate women, he is really afraid of his unconscious nature in which the anima rules. In an age that was characterized by one-sided attitudes, it was natural that there was a good deal of so-called male chauvinism. On the other hand, the woman who pursues liberation with rage and vengeance, as is so often the case, is also preventing her own individuation. Liberation from outworn roles and patterns of the past should not lead to animus-possession.

We all need to be liberated, not from each other, but from ourselves—our petty, neurotic, egotistical, one-sided selves. This liberation is not advanced by movements in the social arena, by magazines, rallies, slogans and noise, but by the progressive movement of the soul's expansion within. Let us change what is outworn in the roles of the sexes; such changes have occurred before and will occur again. But let us not universalize our neuroses and exalt them to the false status of causes. If a man has been maltreated in his life by one or several women, it is not the fault of womankind in general. Such a man does not need an antiwoman political movement; he just needs to find the right woman, outside of himself as well as inside. If a woman has been wronged and abused by some men, let her beware of the sour, anti-men attitudes which have surfaced so powerfully in our era. No true reform of society, no authentic improvement of standards and attitudes can ever come from rage, hatred and resentment on the part of anyone. Jung said in *Civilization in Transition*, "One thing, however, is indubitable—the woman of today is under the same process of transition as man. Whether this transition is a historical turning point or not remains to be seen."

What is taking place may very well be a turning point of history. Whether this turn will be fortuitous will depend upon our individual insight. Let us be aware of our responsibilities to the archetypes, for only they will turn historical occasions into benevolent developments that redound to the essential benefit of our spiritual growth.

Archetypes, it would seem, always play a dual role in the psyche; they unite as well as divide. This role is singularly evident in the case of the anima and animus. Men and women are, at root, different; they possess great biological and psychological disparities. At the same time it must also be recognized that these same archetypal differences are the very factors which attract men and women to each other and thus ultimately lead to the discovery of the contrasexual image within each of the sexes. Thus the very distinctions which in our desire for equality and liberation we sometimes tend to deplore are also the wellspring of human growth toward both inward and outward unity. What divides us is also what unites us, and the very causes of our distress and anxiety are also the causes of our excitement and fulfillment. Neither anima nor animus can make a human psyche alone, even as neither male nor female can constitute the human race alone. Both halves are necessary for making a whole of anything, a fact that is certainly also true of human wholeness. It is therefore evident that the advocacy of what sometimes has been called "separatism" in the relations between the sexes is, to say the least, ill-advised from our point of view. To say that one half needs to separate from the other in order to discover its potential, or to be truly free, is little short of rank folly. Since both the biological and the psychological unity of humankind depends on the process of the conjunction between opposites, a separation of the sexes, as advocated by some radical feminists, appears to be contrary to the intentions of both human biology and psychology. An "apartheid" of the sexes, like the apartheid of the races, might be considered undesirable.

To the question, Will the sexes ever be equal? one may answer both in the affirmative and in the negative. One may answer yes because as each of the two halves is equally important for the making of the whole, it must ultimately be recognized both in the psyche and in society that the two partners in the alchemical work of wholeness must face each other as equals, lest the common work itself come to grief. In another sense, one may also answer no to the question, inasmuch as men and women are in reality equal already. Thus equality is not a prize to be won, but rather a condition that already exists, although it is in frequent need of recognition and acknowledgment in society. Men and women do not have to be made equal; rather their psychically ever-present equality must be given outward and effective recognition.

One more important distinction needs to be made— namely, between equality and egalitarianism. There is a world of difference between a conscious, balanced recognition of essential equalities on the one hand, and a bulldozer-like effort at the leveling all differences on the other. Egalitarianism ideally would like to see sexual, social, cultural and economic differences vanish. What is left out of the egalitarian calculation, however, is the fact that differences rather than identities are the catalysts of change, growth and transformation. Egalitarian societies are invariably stagnant, uncreative and dull, while societal structures, offering a wealth of difference and variety, are vital and transformative.

The *real* problem with democratic society is not that there is too much diversity within its framework, but rather that often there is not enough. A democratic society should, and indeed *must*, offer meaningful choices of lifestyles and attitudes to all of its citizens. Enforced stereotypes of femininity or of masculinity do not belong in a world of free men and women. It is more than understandable that many women of our times have come to resent the restrictive feminine roles into which a rigid society forced them. It would be equally understandable if more men would protest against the artificial masculine stereotypes of society as well. Freedom and choice are always inseparable in life, and persons in a free society must be free to choose the ways in which they express their own masculinity and femininity. Stereotypes and unisexual egalitarianism are both dead wrong and incompatible with freedom.

Thus we are led once again to the all-important alchemical ingredient of individual spiritual growth, which is also the essential component of a growth-oriented society. This ingredient is, of course, freedom. When men and women are free to lead their lives according to convention or without convention, to have marriages and other forms of relationships which may be traditional or nontraditional, when all are free to enter trades and professions for which their training and aptitudes may qualify them and when all receive wages for their labors without distinction based on sex —then, and *only then* can human society lay claim to the role which it is ordained to perform. That role is to serve as the alchemical vessel in which the transformative spiritual growth of humanity can be benevolently facilitated.

"There is no morality without freedom," said Jung. We might add that neither is there, or can there ever be, equality without freedom. Human beings are divided by biology, culture, ideology, religion and last, but not least, by gender. From birth we are either male or female, and this condition is simply not subject to change. In a free society, the destiny of men and women is to live together within the context of a shared destiny of spiritual growth. Every woman is, in addition to many other roles and functions, an embodiment of the anima, and as such, she is a priestess, ministering not only to her fellow humans of the masculine gender, but to the entire culture as well. It is not farfetched to say that our culture has to a large extent lost its own anima because of its excessive masculine orientation. The anima of the culture is therefore in need of restoration, or, one might say, the culture is in need of re-animation.

On the other hand, the priestly function of the masculine half of humanity is also important. The presence of a healthy, confident and compassionate animus force in society, as well as in personal relationships, is a most desirable condition indeed. Here the work of the male is manifestly to be found. Man and woman are ordained thus to a mutually complementary holy priesthood, a sacerdotal office of great and sacred implications. If they can manage to unite within their souls and lives the twin virtues of freedom and consciousness, there can be no obstacle strong enough to prevent the exercise of this mission. One cannot hope to conclude with any more meaningful statement, therefore, than the following verse of the great composer Wolfgang Amadeus Mozart:

> Mann und Weib; Weib und Mann,
> Reichen an die Gottheit an!
> (Man and Woman, Woman and Man,
> Together they approximate the Divine!)
>
> *The Magic Flute*

4

Psychology, Gnosis and the New Moralities

Before we can address the so-called new moralities and the perplexities attached to them, we must first arrive at a satisfactory definition of morality. The word "morality" is derived from the Latin word *mos* or *mores*, which denotes customs, manners and habitual acts. In Greek the word *ethos* means roughly character, from which the term "ethics" is derived. Ethics, in turn, is often defined as the study of the standards of conduct and moral judgment. Morality, therefore, is the quality that is said to determine the correctness or incorrectness, the rightness or wrongness of human action, while ethics, or *scientia moralis* (moral science), is the field of study that concerns itself with morality.

Three Traditional Views of Morality

Plato, the father of classical philosophy, felt that humans had four basic questions or perplexities which philosophy had to answer, one of which was the moral, or ethical question. The four questions are: How do I know? (epistemology); What shall I do? (ethics); How shall I be governed in the community? (political science); and What kind of world do I live in? (cosmology). On the question of ethics, Plato held that a rational (ensouled) being determines his or her conduct within the larger context of the nature of the world and the meaning of human life. One finds this context, so Plato said, by way of the apprehension of ideas, which are the reality underlying persons, experiences and other things. Thus in Platonic thought, reason is regarded as the great ethical agency. One must remember that to Plato, "reason" meant very much more than it does to us. It was a sort of higher mind (often called *nous*), which was thought capable of recognizing the nature and meaning of things.

Plato divided the human being into three parts, of which reason, the ethical faculty, was one. A self-controlled or temperate person, said Plato, is one in whom will (the spiritual part), reason (the soul part) and impulses (the physical part) are brought into harmony. The ethics of classical philosophy, including Platonism, Aristotelianism, Stoicism and other post-Socratic classical philosophical schools, are in the main based on this threefold scheme of Plato. Plato was, of course, much more than an outstanding philosopher. There is some evidence that Plato was the principal agent who made public the nonritualized, or theoretical portions of the great mysteries (Eleusinian, Orphic, Dionysian, Isiac and others). It is an intriguing thought to reflect on the possibility that Plato distilled the outer teachings of the mysteries and made them into a philosophy. In any event, Plato's influence was and remains enormous, and his person and teachings were revered into the medieval Christian period, when, so the story goes, he was considered as a candidate for sainthood!

Constrasting to, though running parallel in time with Plato's position is another ethical or moral tradition, Judaism. The Semitic tradition heavily influenced both Christianity and Islam and was, in turn, influenced by Zoroastrianism. Unlike the Greek, the Semitic mind shows a veritable obsession with morality and ethics. To the Greeks, questions of ethics were only one of four important questions at best; however, to the Jews, the moral question was *the* question. One reason for this is the God-concept of the Jews and various beliefs connected with it. Yahweh is said to have concluded a sort of "deal" or treaty with the Jews, in which he obligated himself to care for his people, but only if they obeyed the laws he had given them. A person who failed to live up to his or her side of the covenant was thus not just a wrongdoer, but an enemy of God and of the chosen people. Since the welfare of the people depended on collective rather than merely individual righteousness, the individual's responsibility for moral actions became a matter of obsessive and guilt-ridden meticulousness, often culminating in prolonged states of anxiety occasioned by the prospect of God's wrath and punishment. (When Freud characterized religion as a collective obsessional neurosis, it was this sort of religion he was thinking about!) Not only did the moralistic orientation of the Semitic religion lead to guilt and anxiety, but it also facilitated morally toned phenomena that Jung called "projections of the shadow." The Jews always held that the Law of Moses was applicable first and most to the chosen people, but by implication this law was seen as extending into the universal sphere of humanity at large. Thus, the people of the Old Testament were not only prone to condemn themselves with considerable frequency, but they also sat in judgment over the moral standards of their "pagan" neighbors.

Thus we find two great moral traditions coexisting in the ancient world: the classical Greco-Roman philosophical tradition based on Plato, and the Semitic tradition based on the Torah. The Greco-Roman tradition holds that reason, or the higher mind, must find its own ethic, as it were; the Semitic tradition says that God has given a law, which must be followed to the letter or even beyond, otherwise dire punishments await both the individual and the people.

When a new development, Christianity, came about, it did a peculiar thing. It proclaimed a new dispensation, a new age, with a consequently new attitude toward ethics and morality. There is very little doubt that for all intents and purposes, Jesus openly renounced or abrogated the Law of Moses, and for this offense, he was killed. Both canonical and Gnostic gospels contain numerous references to Jesus proclaiming new commandments and encouraging people to break the old ones. However, as Christianity grew, it did not always find it convenient to adhere openly to this antinomian or libertarian program.

As one might expect, the ancient people who were most faithful to the libertarian example Jesus set were the Gnostics. They delighted in declaring the Mosaic Law defunct, and they openly violated its commandments, to their own delight, and to the consternation of the pious. In general terms, and especially in terms of what could be called their protopsychology, the Gnostics were in agreement with Plato, although they gave the Platonic model a new and somewhat different twist. To the three parts of the human being mentioned by Plato—namely, will, reason and impulses—they opposed another three-part model, consisting of spirit, soul and matter (or material body). The Gnostics said, in effect, that while Plato was right in saying that there are three parts to the human psycho-physiological organism, he was, at the same time, not very realistic in assuming that reason is strong enough to cause human beings to exercise self-control and to render them temperate. Rather, they seemed to say, people have differing moral capacities which can be classified according to three different types.

The psychological typology established by the Gnostics differentiates between persons ruled by spirit (pneumatics), those ruled by soul (psychics) and those ruled by the material impulses (hyletics). It might be said that the Gnostics represented a psychological orientation in constrast to Plato's pure philosophical idealism. The Gnostics said that everyone does not come to the same conclusion as to what is right and what is wrong because everyone does not perceive reality in the same manner. One's perception of reality, whether moral reality or any other, depends on one's spiritual development. While Plato looked for the criteria of morality in ideas, and the Semitic religion looked for it in the Law of Moses, the Gnostics held that these criteria are in the person.

Thus we now have three constrasting moral positions: the Platonic, the Jewish and the Gnostic. Let us compare them further. The Platonic view holds that reason must be cultivated, because reason is able to contemplate the true ideas which abide beyond earthly things. By way of reason, individuals will be able to express the true, spiritual will and rule over the lower impulses. The Semitic position states that there is one God who has one law which must be followed by all. The Gnostics brought in the notion that right action comes only with the right state of consciousness, or Gnosis. Only those who are in authentic contact with their spiritual nature can be said to be morally right; anything short of this authentic contact carries within itself the seeds of imperfection. Thus, while Plato centered his moral or ethical sense in reason, the Gnostics identified it rather with spirit, the highest of the three constituent parts of the human being. Significantly, the Gnostics also declared that morality depends on consciousness, and that one cannot expect the same level of morality from an unconscious person as one can from a partially conscious individual or from a fully conscious person—the true pneumatic Gnostic.

The Gnostics generally understood that the unconscious, or material person was in need of a moral code appropriate to his or her condition, and the partially conscious, or psychic person was in need of a moral code that was appropriate to this status. Similarly, the pneumatic, or true Gnostic, who received moral inspiration directly from the spiritual nature, was in turn entitled to live according to his or her inspired pneumatic ethic. (This view was known to the common sense of the ancient world. It was embodied in the popular Latin proverb, "What is permissible for Jupiter is not permissible for the ox.")

As is well-known, the Gnostics were forced off the stage of history about the third century, and their ethic did not endure, at least not on a popular scale. What endured and, while battered and dilapidated, is still with us, is the morality of mainstream Christianity. This moral tradition might be described as a curious patchwork composed of many elements, but without a central core of either reason or spirituality. Jewish law, Christian lore, Platonic idealism, Aristotelian rationalism and other elements all eventually entered Christian moral theology, as have astonishing additions, including the predestination theory of the reformer Calvin. As is inevitable, this moral theology was combined with a cosmology which was a similar crazy quilt of heterogeneous ideas and traditions.

The Breakdown of Traditional Morality

For a while all went well, but beginning with the Renaissance, Christian cosmology, as well as morality, began to break down, and the process of deterioration has gone on ever since. As Gerald Heard pointed out in his seminal trilogy on morals (*Morals Since 1900; Pain, Sex and Time* and *The Third Morality*) and as I noted in Chapter 1, such figures as Copernicus, Galileo, Machiavelli, Newton, Darwin and finally Sigmund Freud drove increasingly larger wedges into the cosmological and ethical structure of traditional mainstream Christianity. The latest and in some ways greatest of destroyers in this respect was undoubtedly Freud. Freud denuded the inmost recesses of the soul of the presence, real or imagined, of the Divine spark, and in its place he enthroned the instinctual libido. In effect, Freud said, there is no God; there is no soul; there is only a relatively frail conscious ego trying to hold its own against the great sexual forces of the unconscious. And he should have concluded by adding, and may God, who does not exist, have mercy on your psyche, which is a hopeless mess!

Freud's message was dynamite to the culture, and he was not entirely unaware of this effect. Freud was a curious individual, conservative, middle class, unadventurous and lacking in romance and imagination in many areas of life. Despite all his talk about sex and libido, he was very much attached to conventional and traditional taboos and shibboleths, and like all conventional people, he habitually and furtively broke some of these. Like many nineteenth century atheistic humanists, he also nourished the weird notion that ethics, divorced from metaphysics and cosmo-conceptual elements (*Weltanschauung*), could survive in humanity. He saw nothing contradictory in the notion that people could live without a spiritually-based cosmology and set of values and still remain well-behaved and temperate members of civilized society.

Jung had a different orientation. Like the ancient Gnostics, Jung was of the opinion that what was essential for real morality was not so much an external framework as an internally transformed consciousness. As early as 1910, Freud and Jung argued about the foundations of morality and the role of morality in human life. Freud defended the notion of rules and laws as absolutely essential safeguards of civilization, while Jung said that the important issue was raising human consciousness to a level of being where it would naturally partake of a high ethical and moral character. Jung was restating in modern psychological and, at times, philosophical terms what the ancient Gnostics knew to be true some eighteen hundred years earlier— namely, that true ethics, or real existential morality, arises only from transformation, and that all else is really a substitute, what in German is aptly called *ersatz*. Freud had vague notions that people ought to learn how to behave, while Jung had a far less vague idea that people ought to grow and become pneumatics —transformed spiritual beings. Then their moral perplexities would end.

Freud became a much more influential force in the culture than Jung. His ideas were disseminated widely, and due to their popularization and, often, bowdlerization, they caused quite a bit of havoc and mayhem in society. Freud, who was rather a Victorian paterfamilias personally, would have been amazed had he known of the curious ways in which his ideas led to an era of excessive permissiveness in child rearing and education. The reasoning behind these excesses ran as follows: No one is really responsible, for everyone is a victim of the great monster, the unconscious. Punishment of any kind is therefore unjustified. Nasty, cruel and degrading acts are not really performed by criminals, but by troubled victims of their unconscious. (Add to this argument a bit of Marxist spice, and criminals become not only the victims of their unconsciousness, but of evil capitalist society, a demon even more monstrous than the Freudian unconscious.) Repression in Freudian eyes is evil, and therefore discipline is evil also. Thus we must discipline as little as possible, lest we repress.

One Freudian concept which became a social bombshell was adjustment. Freud taught that the ego has to adjust to the external reality, and if it fails to do so successfully, the person becomes a neurotic. From this concept, the popular pseudo-psychology of educational theorists deduced that education must be utilized primarily for the purposes of social adjustment. To these theorists, it matters little whether schoolchildren learn anything while in school; the important thing is that the school promotes children's social adjustment. The school becomes a social incubator (to use a term coined by the late Robert M. Hutchins) in lieu of a place of learning. It becomes more important for young persons to have a social experience in school than to master even the most elementary learning skills, and even less to absorb even a modicum of the great heritage of Western culture. Without discipline, without a sense of values, without essential skills of the mind, without a refinement of their feelings, several generations have now grown up under the disastrous umbrella of educational guidelines influenced by Freudian psychology or its popularized applications. Much valuable psychic material has been lost to the culture. And what has been gained? Are people better adjusted? No. Are they less neurotic? Decidedly not. Are they less prone to crime and mental illness? No. Are they happy? No. Are they healthy in mind or body? No. The ledger shows much on the debit side, and little on the credit side. The Freudian influence on our culture has been one big disaster!

And what of Jung? Always the true Gnostic, he continued to insist that the one important thing is for us to become conscious. Then, by knowing—by Gnosis, as the ancients would have said—we can rise not only above our impulses and imperfections, but above the shackles of ordinary morality itself. In *C. G. Jung Speaking*, Jung's disciple, Esther Harding, quotes Jung from her notebooks as saying:

> If we are conscious, morality no longer exists. If we are not conscious, we are still slaves, and we are accursed if we obey not the law. He [Jung] said that if we belong to the secret church, then we belong, and we need not worry about it, but can go our own way. If we do not belong, no amount of teaching or organization can bring us there.

Here we have the old, much abominated elitism of the Gnostics. But what of it? Can there be a moral equality? Can there be a morality that is equal and applicable to all? The answer is that such a thing cannot be. People are equal in ultimate spiritual potential, but they are anything but equal in actual development. Not all people are conscious; in fact, few are. Some are only partially or occasionally conscious, and many, many are very unconscious. There are today, just as there were long ago in Alexandria and other Gnostic cities, people who are materialists or hyletics. They are in need of swift justice, of physical deterrents to crime, of punishment rather than rehabilitation. There are in our days also, people at the psychic level who are people of the law and of the book. They need a code, a system, whether written by Moses or by Kant or Hume, which will guide them. The believers must believe, so that by believing they may live in peace and order. In God's good time, they will perhaps come to the place where they may know, and then they will not need to believe any longer. Until then, let them worship their laws and live by them as best they can. And, assuredly, there are today also pneumatics—Gnostics, those who know, those who are conscious. They have outgrown the law; indeed, they are the true law embodied. They hear the command within, daily, hourly, and thus they have little need of commandment. These are the men and women who have come out of great tribulations, painful and stressful existential encounters, hard, perilous moral choices, and who have, nevertheless, prevailed. They are those, who, in the words of Jung, truly "belong to the secret church," the great cathedral of the interior Gnosis. Jung was such a man, and there are others. They are the salt of the earth, and more than that, they are the living philosophers' stones.

Freedom and the New Morality

Did this chapter say anything about new moralities? Perhaps it did, and perhaps not. It really does not matter much. The so-called new moralities are not really new. While some counterproductive and silly elements will no doubt surface in these new moralities, they are essentially a healthy sign. Sexual promiscuity, experimentation with unworkable alternative lifestyles and generally irresponsible behavior have been known to accompany changes in the moral climate of the culture. It seems best to take such phenomena in stride and to regard them as shadows accompanying the light of freedom. Once again we are discovering that it is unwise and unhealthy to demand that all people live by a common, unalterable moral code. Some common agreements must be reached regarding public morality, of course, but these agreements should be based on expediency rather than on considerations derived from Mount Sinai or its equivalent. Private morality should be private and free. In this way, the different soul types will naturally find their particular moral niches in a wise and free society and will grow spiritually and morally at their own pace and in their own way. A truly pluralistic society would of necessity be a Gnostic society. It would be neither anarchical nor tyrannical, neither egalitarian nor elitist, but free. The freedom envisioned here is not freedom to live according to someone else's code, but rather the freedom to choose, to experiment, to grow and also to fail. We do not belong to Jehovah; neither do we belong to Uncle Sam, but to ourselves. Liberty in the true sense is the sole guarantee of an ultimately meaningful and useful life; there is no other. And, repeating once again the words of Jung, "There is no morality without freedom," let us address ourselves to the imperative of moral freedom.

5

The Psychology and Mysticism of Tyranny

Before beginning our discussion of the nature of tyranny, it may be useful to define our terms. As noted in Chapter 1, the ancient Greeks, from whom a great many concepts relevant to our own political and governmental systems are derived, distinguished between three forms of government. One of these was aristocracy, rule by the best; the second was democracy, rule by the people or by the lower strata of the people; and the third was tyranny, or *tyrannis*, as it was called in Greek.

Of these three, the aristocratic form of government was favored by most philosophers and other outstanding persons in Greece. Democracy was regarded as rather undesirable, and tyranny was regarded as even more undesirable than democracy. Of course, we must remember that in the case of democracy, the concept and the reality described by the concept have changed since the time of the Greek city-states.

However, the Greeks were most opposed to tyranny, which they distinguished from kingship, a fourth form of government known to the ancients. Kingship, a monarchical form of government, implied rule by one person, *monos*, but not in a tyrannical manner. By tyranny, the Greeks meant the unrestrained rule or over-lordship of one person, who is not placed into his or her position of authority by any preordained or lawful process, and who is not restrained in the exercise of power by any other agency but individual judgment. The Greeks considered this kind of an unrestrained influence or rule by one individual to be very injurious to the welfare of the body politic.

The Roman attitude toward these matters was somewhat different in the days of the Republic. In ordinary and peaceful times, the government was headed by an elected co-rulership of two persons called the consuls. However, as soon as a national emergency arose, the Romans elected a dictator. The Romans would have agreed with Napoleon, a dictator who stated many centuries later that particularly in difficult times, one head, even though mediocre, is preferable for rulership to the compromises of any number of excellent heads. As soon as the national emergency was over, the Romans tried, not always successfully, to get rid of the dictator; however, then, as now, dictators had a proclivity for hanging on to the power they assumed.

Like the Romans, we have experienced throughout history the establishment of tyrannies, arising out of many diverse governmental systems. This process is not foreign to our present age, as it was not foreign to humanity throughout history. At the present time and within comparatively recent history, we have seen primarily two forms of tyrannical government. One kind of tyranny is primarily psychological in content, while the other, while psychological in its inception, often maintains its power primarily by rational, organizational means. Of these the first type is more interesting, and we shall investigate this variety in depth because its psychological overtones and spiritual and quasi-religious aspects are significant.

In the psychological kind of tyranny, a tyrant appears as the exponent of a great, powerful and usually suddenly unleashed psychological development or movement. If we look upon tyranny as something undesirable, we might say that the tyrant is the principal symptom, as well as, to some extent, the continuing pathogenic agency—as one would call it in medicine—of a psychic epidemic.

Such tyrannies are usually extremely dramatic. They possess considerable popularity, at least for a period of time, and they represent a mysterious, disturbing and ultimately frequently disastrous outburst of peculiar and uncontrollable psychological forces in a people. Even in a secular age, and even under circumstances in which the traditional or established symbols of religion are no longer used, this kind of tyranny has a primarily religious character, if we understand "religious" to mean relating to the nonrational, deep unconscious of the human psyche.

The most recent and most momentous example of this kind of tyranny was the rule of Adolf Hitler and his party, the NSDAP, or National-Sozialistische-Deutsche-Arbeiter-Partei (the National Socialist German Workers Party). The type of tyranny exemplified by Hitler is the most dramatic and usually the most destructive variety.

The second form of tyranny is somewhat similar to the first, but though a psychological condition or predisposition may come about in a people or a nation which causes the tyranny to be established, the tyranny does not possess such a monumental psychological charge and power as the first type. After some time, the psychological charge begins to evaporate, and the tyranny continues to maintain itself by way of a rational, manipulative organizational procedure and force. In my view, this kind of tyranny is represented today by the still remaining Communist one-party rule governments throughout the world, such as the People's Republic of China, Cuba, North Korea and Vietnam. In none of these countries can we speak of a real psychic epidemic of the magnitude and character that the Nazi German phenomenon represented.

In such cases we are faced not with a true psychic epidemic, but rather with a temporary and rather short-lived psychic flareup. It then becomes institutionalized by a group, a tyrannical oligarchy of sorts, which then maintains itself in power, often for a long time.

Two Types of Tyrants

To illustrate, let us compare Mussolini, Hitler and Stalin. Mussolini was a bit of a clown along with everything else, and you can never totally condemn a clown, because it has at least some entertainment value. His dictatorship appears to have been a hybrid of the two types of tyranny discussed. But if you compare, for instance, the figure of Iosip Vissarionovich Stalin with Adolf Hitler, you will find that they are totally different. Both have produced frightful phenomena in history and have brought untold suffering and death to large numbers of people, but in quite different manners and out of different motives.

Hitler was swept along by uncontrollable forces of a mysterious psychological nature within himself and flowing forth from the psyche of his people. He rode the crest wave of these forces as long as the psychic storm lasted. And as soon as the psychic storm died down, as it were, Hitler's power—I don't mean the external power of force, or terror, of armies and weapons, but his interior power to govern and to do what he wanted to do —was gone. So that one can look at the history of World War II and one can pinpoint the time when Hitler's fortunes began to reverse themselves—when he was no longer filled with that peculiar, evil, impulsive, but really artistic, inspiration which guided him in the earlier period of his career. Hitler began to lose touch with the "god" of inspiration and power at the time when the psychic epidemic in the German people began to subside; when this happened, he no longer was in tune with the great, powerful forces of the unconscious of his people. One needs to keep in mind that Hitler came to power and maintained himself in power for a considerable period of time by way of the manifest will of the overwhelming majority of the German people. Hitler was a popular ruler until about 1942, give or take a year. So there are popular tyrants. Tyranny and popularity are not exclusive by any means.

Now, in contrast to Hitler is the figure of Stalin—a coldly rational individual at all times, totally in control of his own thinking, of his own feelings; diplomatic, clever and, with the exception of the last years of his life, extremely realistic in his appraisal of all circumstances within his domain. This was an individual who wiped out and caused to be butchered millions of people, not because of some kind of weird, emotional obsession that has to do with a racial mythos, but because of a totally cold, calculating mentality which declared a particular course of action to be to his advantage and to the advantage of the cause which he represented.

We find, of course, that along with these larger-than-life exponents of tyrannical systems, there are others which fall in between these categories, but which have a certain relationship to one or the other. For example, we find a lot of dictatorships and tyrannies in Latin America and in Third World countries. The same is true in various places where power is exercised by people who are either leaning a little bit in the direction of psychological dictatorship or, on the other hand, are mere manipulators of power, who in a calculating and rational manner, wish to maintain themselves in a ruling position.

The Tyranny of Hitler

Since the psychological overtones and aspects of government are more relevant to our discussion of freedom, I shall concentrate in what follows on the tyranny of Hitler. Hitler is regarded, not without good reason, by many people as the embodiment of monumental evil. He was guilty of precipitating the greatest and the most devastating world war to date, and also was the tyrant who caused a holocaust wiping out millions of people. All of this he accomplished within a relatively short but very intense period of time. The "Thousand Year Reich" endured for not much more than fifteen years. And yet within this short period of time, Hitler managed to accomplish the greatest conflagration and slaughter, both foreign and domestic, known in the history of any country. This puzzled people, and it still does. It amazes particularly the people who were not present in the area where it occurred, although even those who were are puzzled by it to a large extent.

It is difficult to accept that a phenomenon such as Hitler was of an entirely mundane and natural character. It is mind-boggling to contemplate that such massive carnage could happen, and therefore the suggestion arises very easily in the mind that some unusual, supernormal, abnormal or perhaps even supernatural factors must have been involved or at work. And, indeed, more and more literature seems to promote that point of view. Very often in the history of the world when we see someone whom we regard as particularly evil, we tend to assume that the evil that the person brings into the world is so titanic that it must come from a source beyond the person—that so much evil could not come from a human personality, or even a group of human personalities. We assume, therefore, that something metaphysically diabolical, some sort of satanic evil must be at work.

This is not an unreasonable conclusion in itself—not because I believe in a personal devil with horns and tail, although I sometimes wish I could, because it is an interesting, romantic way of looking at evil. But unfortunately, we can't really link up the kinds of devilry that went on in Germany at that time with the conventional kind of romantic devils. There was really something else at work. In essence, everyone has his or her own devil, and when people consigned Old Nick to oblivion, banishing him into the Dark Ages, they had to start inventing their own devils. Of course Hitler had his devils —the Jewish people. He needed them exceedingly because on the back of that hatred, that antagonism, that propaganda, to a large extent, he rode to power. Many people have their particular devils in that way.

Later, in occult and metaphysical circles, there arose a myth concerning Hitler's black magic, or Hitler's devilry. This notion was primarily documented by a curious compendium of ideas called *The Spear of Destiny*, by the English writer Trevor Ravenscroft. This little book hit the world like a peculiar bombshell

about 1973, causing a considerable amount of excitement. Ravenscroft was not alone in his attempt to explain the phenomenon of Hitler in terms of a weird,
evil, occult mythos. He was inspired and preceded by a
few others, most immediately by the French writer
Jean-Michel Angébert, whose book *Hitler et la Tradition Cathare, Hitler and the Cathar Tradition*, was
translated into English under the title *The Occult and
the Third Reich*. Angébert's book apparently gave
Ravenscroft an idea for how to concoct an interesting
mythos.

Jean-Michel Angébert writes according to a genre
that has existed for a long time, particularly in France.
The French have a tradition in which people write
books ostensibly with one point of view, which at the
same time covertly serve a different purpose, often the
opposite one. In Angébert's book, the notion is brought
forth that Hitler had gotten into the possession of the
Holy Grail, which prior to that time had been in the
possession of the Cathars. According to Angébert, the
Grail was found by a German archaeologist in a cave in
the Pyrenees and spirited back to Germany. Clearly
Angébert's wild thesis inspired the recently popular
movie *Indiana Jones and the Last Crusade*, which
follows this plot exactly, except for the ending.

Trevor Ravenscroft added to the myth by saying that
along with the Grail, Hitler possessed various other
magical objects such as a lance or a spear. He revised
Angébert's thesis to refer to a spear, which he called
"The Spear of Destiny." Ravenscroft's spear didn't have
to come out of the mountains in the Pyrenees; instead, it
was reposing in one of the glorified junk rooms of the
Imperial Museum in Vienna, where I have been a few
times. I may have even seen the spear or its facsimile,
because I visited a room in the Hof Museum in Vienna

where were kept the *Reichskleinodien*, which means "Imperial trinkets." Among them was a great deal of sacred junk including the spurious Spear of Longinus, rechristened by Ravenscroft as The Spear of Destiny.

To put it briefly, the thesis propounded by Ravenscroft was that the spear, which held great occult powers, had fallen into the hands of Hitler. By way of this object of power, he was able to accomplish all of the evil things that he did. Ravenscroft added all kinds of obfuscations and deliberate confusions about occult influences in Hitler's life. For instance, Ravenscroft claimed that a large number of German politicians, statesmen and political roustabouts, who at one time or another had some connection with the Nazi party, were involved in occult or quasi-occult activity.

This idea is plausible because the period between the two world wars was in some ways rather similar to our own. There was a considerable upsurge of occult and metaphysical interest in Europe and particularly in Germany in that period; organizations and individual teachers abounded, from the more respectable and interesting, such as Dr. Rudolf Steiner, to some really very sleazy folk, such as Lanz von Liebenfels and General Erich Ludendorff. And so it is easy to find individual persons in Hitler's entourage, or in some connection with the Nazi party, who were involved in occult studies.

Going clear back into World War I, the Chief of the Imperial General Staff, Count Helmut Von Moltke, the younger, was a close associate and disciple of Rudolf Steiner. Moreover, General Moltke was quite convinced that he had a number of previous incarnations, which he freely talked about. No wonder he didn't last very long in his position in World War I. Several other prominent Germans also had occult involvements, like Professor Karl Haushofer, a former general who became a professor at the University of Munich. He was noted for his formulation of both the term and idea of geopolitics. Others included Dietrich Eckart of the German Workers Party, the predecessor of the Nazi party, and many others. But none of these data of course prove in any way that Hitler's activities were based on sorcery in the traditional sense of the term.

Hitler's Sorcery

In my view, Hitler had a sorcery, but it was of a different nature than what Ravenscroft implied. There were two factors involved in the kind of sorcery that Hitler represented. One, that might be called in a sense positive, was the sorcery of Hitler's magical personality. Hitler was one of those charismatic individuals who was capable of infusing large numbers of people with ideas and convictions which under ordinary circumstances they would have resisted. There is absolutely no doubt that this was so. He had a tremendously magical personality, who at the same time was personally unprepossessing. He was by no means handsome, but rather shabby and scrawny in appearance, with a voice that was not particularly sonorous or euphonious and with a command of the German language which was anything but cultured. He spoke German with an Austrian accent, and a rather vulgar one at that. There was very little in the man that would recommend him to the public. Yet, once he got on the platform, shouting and screaming in a fashion that would have caused an audience to walk out under other circumstances, he enthralled and convinced and magically transformed people in a most astonishing fashion. This was the result of what one may call the "positive" force emanating from Hitler.

On the other hand, there was also a "negative" magical aspect to Hitler, because he was able to galvanize in a magical fashion the negative projections of dislike, hatred and antagonism from the depths of the unconscious of a very large number of people. He evoked, as it were, the very devils, the very demons that, in their unconscious, people wanted to hate; he moved people by way of these particular negative forces. The noted German historian of recent times, Ernst Nolte, called Hitler, without any qualification or modification, a *medium*. By this Nolte implied not necessarily a spiritualistic meaning of that term, but rather the ability of an individual to become the channel for the ordinarily repressed and suppressed unconscious forces of large masses of people. By way of the combination of all of these factors, Hitler became the unbelievable, psychologically inspired tyrant of the age.

As a matter of bizarre interest we might also mention that the literature which forever hunts for occult angles to Hitler's activities has even managed to link Hitler, without any valid evidence whatsoever, with the then aged Russian magus residing in France, George Ivanovich Gurdjieff. A Frenchman, Louis Pauwels, at one time a disciple of Gurdjieff, was antagonized by Gurdjieff. Pauwels ran away from Gurdjieff and subsequently, either consciously or unconsciously, wanted to take revenge on the old man by writing books in which he linked Gurdjieff with just about every kind of nefarious activity that exists in the world. Pauwels eventually wrote a book that was also quite popular both in Europe and America, coauthored with Jacques Bergier, called *The Morning of the Magicians* or *The Dawn of Magic*. The book threw journalistic dust into the eyes of the public by implying that somehow from his lonely and impecunious exile in a suburb of Paris, Gurdjieff had manipulated Hitler and told him what to do. The notion is, of course, quite preposterous. Many weird stories about Hitler have circulated in this fashion. What we need to remember is that there was indeed in Hitler's case, as there very frequently is, valid sorcery. The phenomenon was of a magical nature, but the magic and the sorcery was not of the type fantasized and projected by these people in their books. It was of a much more direct but also a much more devastating nature.

The Example of Germany

What actually happened in Germany? What kind of psychological motivating force brought the tyranny of Hitler to the top? Hitler did not need to invoke demons after the fashion of classical magicians. The evocation was done for him by the forces of history. The example of Germany is, I think, one which we all should consider with a great deal of seriousness and to our essential profit. More than any other nation or any other people, the German Empire came to be dominated in its education, in its public life, in its official state churches and in its religious life by the forces of rationalism, of law and order. Beginning with the unification of the German nation and the establishment of the Hohenzollern Empire by Bismarck, this was the course that Germany adopted, beginning with the late nineteenth century. The romantic, poetic, feeling-toned aspect of the German soul, its attraction to the dark mysteries of being—the Faustian urge, as various German literary and philosophical figures have called it—was gradually driven underground. Consequently, titanic forces of emotional power built up in the unconscious of the German people. Reason ruled. Efficiency ruled. Order ruled. Peace—at least internal peace, for there was always a militaristic framework to reinforce order—ruled, but underneath it all, titanic emotional forces were seething.

Then the circumstances of history intervened. With the defeat of the so-called central powers (Germany, Austria-Hungary and the Ottoman Empire) at the end of World War I, the entire established structure, with all of its physical and psychological power, was destroyed. The German empire fell. Emperor William II went into exile in Holland, and the entire system crumbled, with a great deal of assistance from outside. What was particularly significant was the destruction of the symbols of authority, the symbols of order and of reason. A tremendous psychological vacuum was created. The controls which had held the forces of the unconscious in check for such a long time were no longer there. After a relatively brief period of floundering, the German unconscious, the demons of the netherworld, the old Gods, as Carl Jung called them, the old warlike, cruel, uncultured, destructive, Nordic, Germanic gods of the pre-Christian era, symbolically speaking, burst forth from the earth and took over the minds, the psyches of the people. And as it inevitably happens, at such a time, a human exponent of these forces arose. The unconscious forces, the archetypes, the gods, if you wish to call them that, will always find their exponent, their medium, their mouthpiece. And the principal mouthpiece for these forces was, of course, Adolf Hitler.

The ways in which Hitler operated, particularly during the period when he was still successful, are psychologically very interesting. Hitler was totally incapable of, and unwilling to do any kind of systematic, organized labor. In this respect he was very different from the rest of the German people. His was a Bohemian, artistic temperament. He was an unsuccessful artist who, because of his inability to break into or excel in the artistic world, was more or less a tramp most of his life, a hobo, a derelict, until he went into the Army during World War I and then, after that, into politics. Yet, with this totally unorganized and unsystematic lifestyle and mode of thinking, Hitler was capable of an unbelievable creative intuition for his own purposes. People who knew him, people in his entourage, would say that when important decisions had to be made, Hitler would procrastinate for days or weeks. He would walk around in his quarters, usually in his mountain retreat in Berchtesgaden and work himself up into a very nervous state. He had a terrible temper. He was terribly unhappy and was subject to incredible fits of depression and confusion during this time. Something was obviously boiling and churning within him. And then, all of a sudden, he would come out of his room, his eyes cleared up, his facial expression changed. He had reached the decision; it had come to him. Then he moved with lightning speed, giving commands to everyone all down the line. And then, of course, his magnificently organized military and political machinery carried out his decision.

While Hitler was able to operate and function in this fashion, he was unbelievably successful in everything that he undertook. When the war, particularly the Russian campaign, began to mount, he was forced, more or less against his better judgment, by his Army officers and his generals, to set up a military headquarters, because after the fashion of the real tyrants, he had done away with the various traditional offices of the army that had existed prior to his coming to power. He could not delegate authority. He fired the commander in chief of the armed forces and concentrated the supreme authority within himself. For this reason he now had to subject himself to a certain form of military discipline. He had to move to a general headquarters. He had to hold regular staff meetings. He had to keep regular business hours. Interestingly, as soon as Hitler did this, his decisions and his strategies started to go wrong. And the longer he stayed in the military routine, which went contrary to his artistic and weirdly intuitive, perhaps even psychotic way of doing things, the less success he had. In a nutshell, that is really how Adolf Hitler lost the war.

So in Hitler we really have a demonic, mediumistic personality, highly neurotic, but at the same time tremendously responsive to the underlying psychological forces, who while he was able to function in his own fashion, served his own purposes and cause with tremendous efficiency. When he was unable to do that anymore, he began to lose ground.

One of the very few people who recognized this peculiar psychic, demonic character of the Nazi tyranny was Carl Jung. Because of Jung's insight into Hitler, he has been wrongfully accused of having been a Nazi sympathizer. The accusation also had something to do with Jung's desire to save the psychoanalytic movement at the time when the Nazis obtained supremacy in Germany. Since Jung was the only leading person in the depth psychology movement at that time who was not Jewish, he tried to hold on to the position of leader of the international and German Psychoanalytic Association, and to the post of editor of its journals. But Jung very soon found that one could not do that sort of thing without becoming totally enslaved by the Nazi government; thus he resigned his position. He even had a very unpleasant personal encounter with German propagandist Dr. Joseph Goebbels, which ended in a shouting match. Jung was one of the very few people, I think, who told Goebbels off and got away with it. But then, of course, Jung was Swiss, too, and a fairly important Swiss, so he was protected to some extent.

Thus in the case of National Socialist Germany, we are faced with a peculiar and mysterious psychological phenomenon from which we can learn. What can we learn from it? For one thing, I think we can learn that highly trained, highly educated countries and peoples of a high cultural level—people well schooled, well educated, well acquainted with the high culture of their particular country, with disciplined minds, with indoctrinated character traits of thrift, industry and logic—can be victimized in very short order by psychological forces that are totally contrary to these qualities and can be swept off their feet not only in the smaller numbers of tens or hundreds or thousands, but by the ten millions, and if necessary, by the hundreds of millions. If this phenomenon was possible then, it is possible now. Psychic epidemics can and do occur, not only in Germany. Given this, how does one prevent the occurrence of similar psychic epidemics?

Preventing Psychic Epidemics

Jung believed that a people whose psyche is lacking in efficient modalities to integrate the opposites of culture, the opposites of psychological forces, the opposites of emotion and feeling and thinking is very, very vulnerable to psychic epidemics, even as an individual with similar characteristics is extremely vulnerable psychologically. When the external controls are too many, and the controlled forces within are restive, the inner restraints eventually will give way. Even if World War I had not ended in a disaster for Germany, even if the power structure and the symbols had not been destroyed and the tremendous worldwide economic depression had not come, the chances are that some sort of an outburst, some sort of an epidemic of the soul, would have taken place in Germany—perhaps not of the disastrous magnitude that we saw in Hitler, but something drastic would certainly have happened.

Thus we need to revise our dangerous and unfortunate assumption that we can run life at the personal or at the collective level of society, through a one-track mentality, possessing only a conscious direction. The entire pattern of our thinking, our one-sidedness, our excessive orientation toward purely conscious goals, must be submitted to a substantial modification if we are to survive. We must also recognize that behind this one-sidedness, this unresponsiveness to the promptings of unconscious forces, stand ancient and deadly archetypal forces that hold us in their grip, even as we deny our allegiance to them. It sounds unreasonable to say that Hitler or Stalin were really suffering from a "Jehovah complex" and were manipulated by religious forces. These men consciously denied their dependence on the gods, or on God. But that which they denied was using them nevertheless! Symbolic realities of a religious nature dwelt behind their differing but still alienated and one-sided psychological attitudes. These realities were expressed in their conduct of affairs of state. Both leaders manipulated and ordered about empires of many millions, but they in turn were commanded and directed by archetypal symbols from within their being, although less in the case of Stalin and more in that of Hitler.

The present world shows ample evidence of the rule of symbols as well. Look, for example, at the Islamic world today. The power that the Islamic revolutions of Iran and various other places possess is purely founded on religious thinking and in very powerful archetypal symbols, which the leaders know how to manipulate expertly in order to rule the masses. While the presence of religious symbolic forces is particularly evident in cases of outright theocratic tyrannies, such as the Islamic states, we must also recognize that similar factors are at work in other places. Religious origins lie behind the circumstances of most modern tyrannies, whether they be of Fascist, Communist, Islamic or any other ideological motivation.

And what may these forces and origins be? We are not able to analyze them all here, but we may mention at least one, which is particularly pertinent. Ideological tyrannies inevitably have a great relationship to the model of a unitary, monolithic world image, of the kind that results from the orthodoxies of the great monotheistic world religions, Christianity, Judaism and Islam. These are the "one-track mind religions" par excellence. Their worldview declares that there is one God, one truth, one standard of rectitude, one valid revelation, and that it is incumbent upon all persons who are intelligent and interested in the salvation of their souls to accept this one and only, true model of reality. With all their faults, Eastern religions, such as Hinduism, Buddhism and Taoism, do not have this one-track mentality. Actually, the entire model goes back to the covenant concept of Judaism, which, like an archetypal obsession, still dominates the predominantly secularized Christian world as well as the anything but secularized Islamic world.

As the present book has pointed out, there are two

traditions in our culture. The first is the Semitic tradition of the "One God-One Reality" universe, which has been dominant by way of non-Gnostic Christianity since the third century. In spite of the victory of the Nicene Fathers, however, the tradition of the alternative reality and its alternative spirituality continues to exist in a subterranean fashion. As indicated above, the Gnostic worldview is based on opposites or is—to use a dangerously charged term—dualistic. Adherents of this model of reality could easily and naturally envision a pluralistic society, in which peacefully contending political and economic forces interact with each other, to produce new results. The principle of conflict leading to synthesis inherent in elective democracy and free economy was the natural extension of the spiritual model of the Hermetic Gnosis. The European monarchies, in contrast, were founded on the divine right of kings, an idea which emerged from the monolithic worldview of the Semitic religion, as modified by medieval Christianity. Even the monarchs of the era of the Enlightenment could not really envision a society of freely interacting forces; thus, they could only rule, not reign. (This is not to say that the European monarchies may not have had much more affinity to the psychology of their peoples than the alienated shadow-republics established in their place, often with American support.)

Modern tyrannies are thus the heirs of the monolithic worldview of the orthodox Judeo-Christian-Islamic religious archetypes. Hitler may have been in a certain sense an exponent of the old Germanic gods, but his methods in large measure conformed to the one-track mind model of the Jehovah archetype. The ideological tyrannies of Marxist allegiance are also essentially Jehovic. Castro, Lenin and Mao Tse-tung were of the same ilk as the grand inquisitors; they all held that "error has no rights against truth."

The alternative spiritual tradition is by its nature opposed to the tyrannical model of reality, which serves as the archetypal foundation for all modern ideological dictatorships. The alternative tradition has little regard for the One God, does not believe in one revelation or one law, or, for that matter, in one truth. It is a spiritually pluralistic tradition, which is attached to the dual forces working out the patterns of growth and transformation in the world. It is a reality image radically different from the monolithic image of Monotheistic religion. It fosters a reality image which is embodied in the twin principles of free government and free enterprise.

Our world has seen three major varieties of ideological tyranny in recent history: German National Socialism, Soviet Communism and Islamic Theocracy. All of these have variants and satellites, of course, but it is sufficient for us to name the principal models. Each of these dictatorships is founded on the unitary model of reality which descends from the Jehovah archetype. While all three are anti-Christian, and two are anti-religious, all three are in reality nourished by the mightiest archetypal sources of the mainstream religions of Western and Mediterranean culture.

The tradition of alternative spirituality is the major opponent of these tyrannies. The Hermetic, Gnostic, Kabbalistic transmission, espousing as it does the principle of creative dualism, fosters a pluralistic and free attitude toward society and economics. It is no doubt true that numerous Christian fundamentalists fiercely champion free enterprise or some trappings of political freedom, but they cannot truly espouse freedom, because they themselves are in the grip of a slavemaster

God. Conversely, numerous persons who possess an interest in esoteric and Hermetic principles have an unreasoning attraction to socialism and its related ideologies, not realizing that these systems inevitably inhibit the Hermetic principle of the free transformational interaction of opposites. Both fundamentalists who espouse freedom and Gnostics who espouse socialism are guilty of a radical inconsistency. Both need to realize that in order for the Hermetic principle to work, it needs a consistent condition of freedom in all areas of life. In order to participate in the Hermetic process to a total degree, people must be free not only in part, but totally; their freedom must be political, spiritual, economic, sexual, intellectual, artistic, educational and in all other areas. The only limitations on their freedom should be ones brought about by the legitimate and demonstrable rights of other persons. Anything short of this is not true and effective freedom. Only a consistent, uncompromising esteem of freedom can be effective, for only such an attitude expresses the Hermetic principle in an undiluted and uncorrupted fashion.

The Gnostic and the Jungian psychological models of reality are two of the most unambiguous sources of Hermetic libertarianism in our days. The Gnostic approach has been primarily mythological, because it is through myth and symbol that the important principles of life are usually realized. Early Gnostic mythology states that the archons, or rulers of this world, are bent upon preventing human freedom and sovereignty. The archons and demiurges are the representatives of a unitary, monistic and monolithic psychological orientation; therefore, they are tyrants by nature. Modern depth psychology, especially as represented by Jung, agrees with this symbolic statement. One of Jung's greatest achievements was that he recognized the underlying vital connection between Hermetic, alchemical and Gnostic symbolism. Thus he put his finger on a tremendously important truth: the transformational task of Gnosis in the world is by way of the creative interaction and conjunction of opposites. No wonder both Jung and the Gnostics were libertarian and antitotalitarian in their thinking. They could not be otherwise without doing violence to their principles and to their deepest spiritual commitments.

While it may sound trite and unfashionably patriotic, we must state once again that the American republic, with its Hermetic origins and deeply rooted archetypal patterns of an alchemical and Gnostic tradition, is still the greatest hope for freedom in our world. This country is not perfect, of course. Neither is anything else in this imperfect world. The unrealistic notion that earthly institutions can be perfect is another fallacy arising from the orthodox Judeo-Christian theological model. Since God is perfect, so this reasoning runs, God's world ought to be perfect also. The fact is that it isn't. The Gnostics expressed this truth mythologically by saying that the creator of this world is not perfect at all, but rather an imperfect, foolish being, who created a flawed world in the image of his own flaws. Humans, on the other hand, said the Gnostics, are in a sense superior to this creator deity, and therefore they can recreate the world in accordance with their Gnosis. They may not be able to perfect the world, but they certainly can improve it—primarily by improving themselves.

The American republic is still the alchemical vessel of liberty. The system of checks and balances between various forces, such as the opposites of labor and management, conservatives and liberals, democrats and republicans, as well as other polarities, continues to produce the philosopher's stone in the form of continued progress. It is worthy of note that this country has never supported for any length of time either a one-party dictatorship or a multi-party system on the European model. Perhaps the Hermetic archetype underlying the structure of this republic requires a dual arrangement, so that in true alchemical fashion, opposites can interact and combine and thus bring forth new progress. (For a more detailed treatment of this, see Chapter 9.)

As long as the American people keep these principles in mind and alive, as long as they do not permit one of the polarities to take precedence too powerfully and for too long, America will remain a creative alchemical vessel at least in part worthy of its Hermetic foundations. What is required, therefore, is continued vigilance by people in this country and culture to assure the continued effective functioning of the Hermetic vessel or alchemical crucible known as the United States of America. If such vigilance is exercised and implemented, we need fear no tyranny; no evil can take our creative potential and our transformational tasks from us. Our greatest freedom, which justifies all others, is the freedom to become outwardly what we inwardly already are. Thus the only objective worth striving for in our individual or collective life is to have the freedom and the energy, to grow, develop and transform until we approximate the great archetypal paradigm, the Gnostic model of being, implanted in our natures long ago, far away, and indeed out of time and out of this world. And, if we keep these matters in mind and implement them in our actions and lives, we shall be able to repeat in good conscience with Dame Julian of Norwich and with T. S. Eliot that "all shall be well, and all manner of things shall be well."

6

Is Utopia Possible or Necessary?

The dictionary defines "Utopia" as "an ideal common-wealth whose inhabitants exist under perfect conditions." The word itself is Greek; it is composed of *ou*, meaning "not," and *topos*, meaning "a place," thus adding up to *no-place*. This means, of course, that Utopia is no-place, that there is no such place, that Utopia is a place that is not, was not and never will be. The word "Utopia" itself was used first by Sir Thomas More, Lord Chancellor of England and subsequently sainted Catholic martyr, in his book published in 1516 *De Optimo Republicae Statu, Deque Nova Insula Utopia* (Of the Condition of the Best Commonwealth, the New Island of Utopia). More's *Utopia* set a new literary fashion, as it were, and since his time, many Utopian works have been published; some of which were romances, some satires, and some serious philosophical treatises dealing with futuristic hopes for a perfect society. About a hundred years after More's work came *New Atlantis* (1624) by Sir Francis Bacon and *Civitas Solis* (1623) by the Italian Tommaso Campanella.

117

However, the idea of Utopia is far older than Thomas More. It first appears in Plato's *Timaeus* and is further developed in his *Republic*.

What Utopian works have in common is that they all are related to the lost paradise of Atlantis. Atlantis is less a place than an archetypal pattern. Plato recounts the myth of a lost, once-paradisiacal island which sank underneath the waves. Other writers have speculated about such a paradisiacal place, usually an island, but over time increasingly in the sense that such a place might exist in the future rather than that it existed in the past. The psychological development is clear. In Plato's day, the myth of Atlantis was still regarded as a mystery pertaining to the soul—to the psyche rather than to the world. In later times, however, with the increasing differentiation in human consciousness, the paradisiacal Utopia became more and more physical and therefore political. Thus the early phases of psycho-historical development viewed Atlantis or Utopia as past; the more recent ones place it in the future. What does this mean? If Utopia is the Pleroma, the primordial unconscious, then it is obviously of the past—it is the mysterious place of being from which we came. Utopia was once, but is no more; it is under the waves of the unconscious; it is in the great, fathomless sea of mind-stuff. On the other hand, as we come closer to individuation, we come closer to the mysterious land once more. Atlantis rises, and we become aware of the archetype of perfection. In proportion to our increased awareness, we become more apt to project the image of perfection into the world.

When dealing with the contents of the unconscious, we are always faced with three possible courses of action. We may (1) *project* the unconscious; (2) be *possessed* by the unconscious; or (3) if we are particularly aware and fortunate, allow for a *harmonious entry* and *consequent integration* into consciousness of the forces and images dwelling at the unconscious level. These three possibilities have all been used to deal with the unconscious archetype of perfection which we named Utopia.

Perhaps the most frequent course adopted by human minds is projection. We take the image of perfection, the kingdom of heaven within, and project it onto the physical world, in this instance, the political, social and economic world. We want to make society perfect, even as our interior image of wholeness is perfect. We become Utopians, social perfectionists, uncompromising and frequently unrealistic reformers. This is why ideological revolutions and reforms have such a great appeal for some people. They are in reality the projections of our own interior need to reform, to change, to transform. We say, "Change society, change the system, bring down the government, redistribute wealth"; but what we are *really* saying, what the psychological intent of our statements may be said to be, is rather something like, "Change me, transform me, bring down my one-sidedness of consciousness, redistribute my psychic energy, make consciousness available to the neglected portions of myself, to the psychological underdog in myself."

The trouble with projections in general and with the Utopian projection in particular is that such projections work only to a limited degree. Inevitably there comes a time when the projection must be withdrawn. When one falls in love, eventually one must allow the fierce fires of projection to return to their source in the psyche, to leave the love-object with perhaps a certain glow, a residual halo, but not much more. The intensity of projection is useful and normal for a time, in its season, but not indefinitely. Similarly, the Utopian social perfectionist projection must be withdrawn, and a realistic and perhaps even cheerful acceptance of imperfection must come about. Winston Churchill is credited with saying that anyone who is twenty years old and not a revolutionary is abnormal, and that anyone who is sixty years old and not a conservative is a fool. In every situation and in every life, there comes a time when the vision of the ideal must give way to the exercise of the art of the possible. We come to realize that what is easily realizable in the mind is often not at all possible in physical reality. But, we may ask, is this not a cynical position, and, moreover, is it not a view that lacks the kind of romance and excitement that alone make life worthwhile? Are we not depreciating and indeed destroying idealism when we come to such conclusions? The answer, on both counts, is no. Idealism, romance and enthusiasm are valuable and vital qualities of psychic life, but when dealing with concrete, physical realities, ideals and romance suffer an inevitable limitation and frustration. One must contemplate ideals in one's mind, but one must also face facts in the external world. So, we might say, Utopian projections, like all projections must eventually be withdrawn in order to enhance the growth of consciousness.

The second and most undesirable way of dealing with unconscious material is possession. When the ego consciousness is possessed by unconscious content, the consequences are ego inflation, fanaticism, paranoia and megalomania. Inflation and possession of the ego are in and of themselves unhealthy, pathological phenomena. The counterproductive nature of ego inflation and possession is by no means modified or rendered acceptable by the specific character of the unconscious content which brings about the phenomenon. To be possessed by an ideal or a virtue is just as unhealthy as being possessed by the shadow, or one's vices. A fanatic in an evil cause and a fanatic in a good cause are both fanatics, and that is what really matters. Psychologically, when unconscious content possesses the ego and blindly expresses itself by way of the ego, no lasting beneficial results are produced. Consciousness does not grow by way of the unconscious merely living itself out through the conscious structures of the personality. At the very best, such occurrences merely afford the individual a passing psychic relief from the powerful pressures of the unconscious.

Violent revolutions and similar forms of psychic epidemics which occur on a mass scale fall into this category. Whether an anti-Semitic mob becomes possessed by the need to destroy the projected psychological shadow in the form of helpless Jews in a ghetto, or whether a proletarian or peasant mass becomes possessed by the demons of envy and jealousy and burns down a feudal lord's castle, the result is always the same: bloodshed and destruction, with no constructive improvement of anyone's lot. Fanaticism and inflation may masquerade as idealism, but their blind and counterproductive unconscious character is the same. Both obsessive revolutionaries and fanatical reformers are as the colloquialism puts it, "bad news," for both are the victims and the exponents of ego possession.

The last and most desirable alternative to dealing with unconscious material is the orderly, harmonious entry of the unconscious content into consciousness, with consequent interaction of the opposites and their eventual reconciliation and union. From such a union regularly springs new life for the psyche, new solutions to problems and new insights. In the political sphere, we might find an analogue of this alternative in the democratic process of the free rising to expression of the public will, with the consequent interaction of various views of the electorate by political debate, letters, editorials, and other means of free expression by competing political parties. As the process of democratic politics brings divergent and conflicting philosophies of government and various programs of action into creative conjunction, new and beneficial solutions to old problems come about, and the common welfare is advanced. Similarly, within the domain of the marketplace, the free interaction of competing economic forces brings about progress in the spheres of productivity and distribution, to the ultimate benefit of the entire population. Totalitarian governments with managed economies may appear to be efficient for brief periods of time, but in the longer processes of political and economic development, they are inevitably dismal failures, especially when compared with free societies. The economic collapse of the Soviet Union in our day is perhaps the greatest and most convincing example proving this contention. The self-transforming spontaneous order of the human psyche is thus mirrored in, and validated by, the spontaneous alchemy operating in societies possessing political and economic freedom. To conclude the psychological analogy, totalitarian societies and managed economies may be likened to an alienated ego, which is unresponsive to the spontaneous and creative movements of the total psyche. Such an alienated ego desperately holds on to conscious controls, thus preventing the free interaction of psychological opposites and ultimately preventing the emergence of wholeness.

Freeing the Internal Utopia

What does all this say about the perpetual striving of humanity for Utopia? If we recognize that Utopia is really within us, if we know that the image of perfection resides in us right now as a potential, but as yet unconscious wholeness, then it becomes incumbent upon us to allow this internal Utopia to rise to consciousness and to interact with the conscious ego and its world. As always when opposites interact in a creative manner, the result is not the victory of one side over the other. The unconscious Utopia can no doubt contribute to a meaningful modification of the consciously accepted status quo, but it has no realistic prospect of totally overtaking the latter. Similarly, the reality principle, the art of the possible and of expediency, may indeed demonstrate to the total psycho-physiological organism the lack of feasibility of certain aspects of the Utopian vision of the unconscious, but it cannot expect to be immune from the influence of this vision. The two opposites or polarities are destined to interact with each other, and to give birth to a new condition which is not a compromise, but rather a new being, a new creation in its own right. The result of this creative interaction is not unlike the philosopher's stone, which is not the compromise of sulphur and salt, but rather a totally new reality arising from a process of transformation.

Unfortunately, this psychological-alchemical principle is sadly neglected ty Utopians and realists, by liberal socialists and conservative free enterprise advocates. The true difficulty with much of contemporary Utopianism is that it almost inevitably implies that the vision of a few, or even of a sizable number of reformers or revolutionaries, ought to be implemented from the top downward, as it were. Persons who fancy themselves wise, insightful and farseeing, naturally believe that they *know* what is best for everyone; thus they feel that they have a sort of divine right to foist their vision on everyone, making large numbers of people thoroughly miserable in the process. The revolutionary and Utopian zeal of Lenin, Mao Tse-tung, Castro, Hitler, Mussolini or even of the more radical democratic socialist leaders the world over, may be regarded as a one-sided compulsion to externalize certain collective unconscious patterns to the detriment and against the will of the conscious egos of the populations involved. The archetype of the collective unconscious operative in most totalitarian societies and unfree economies is that of the primitive Great Mother in her most lowly, chthonic aspect. "Let Mother State do it for you; and you had better like what she does for you, because ingratitude toward Mother State is evil." Such is the unconscious thinking involved in the ideology of such governmental structures. The independence of the mature offspring of the mother, as demanded by democratic societies and a free economy, is not considered legitimate by Mother State, any more than the sovereignty of grown-up offspring is given due recognition by the tyrannical parents of a family.

On the other hand, the modern conservative or free enterprise system is far less oriented toward the power of government and, therefore, at least in theory, is more open to growth and development from the grassroots, as it were. Obviously, conservative and even libertarian people, being human, will manifest inconsistencies, which in turn are usually the result of unconscious compulsions. Thus, the average conservative looks upon interference in business by the state as evil, but will not similarly condemn interference by the state in the private lives of citizens, particularly in psychologically charged areas such as sexual conduct, abortion or prayer in schools. As noted earlier, one of the difficulties with Utopian ideology in modern times is that when translating itself into political action, it always wishes to impose change from above. Psychologically, we find, however, that truly useful change—change that brings with it authentic progress toward wholeness—never proceeds from above, but rather as a natural growth from below; that is, it arises from the natural alchemy of the union of the opposites. Jung expressed himself on this subject as follows:

> Great innovations never come from above; they come invariably from below; just as trees never grow from the sky downward, but upward from the earth, however, true it is that their seeds have fallen from above. The upheaval of our world and the upheaval in consciousness is one and the same. Everything becomes relative and therefore doubtful. And while man, hesitant and questioning, contemplates a world that is distracted with treaties of peace and pacts of friendship, democracy and dictatorship, capitalism and Bolshevism, his spirit yearns for the answer that will allay the turmoil of doubt and uncertainty.
>
> "The Spiritual Problem of Modern Man" in
> *Civilization in Transition*

The Possibility of Utopia

Is Utopia then possible or necessary? The answer is both yes and no. As an archetype of perfection, a mandala of the unconscious Utopia exists, and thus we possess the ability to envision it consciously. It is also necessary to make contact with this image within ourselves, for like all mandalas, it is a pattern through which our wholeness and ideal totality can be understood and contemplated. On the other hand, Utopia is assuredly not possible as a physical reality in space and time, and to become excessively involved with the idea of its material realization holds great and eminent perils. Things on this earth can assuredly get *better*, but they will never be truly *good;* they can improve, but they never will be perfect. Earthly perfection is an inflation, and when desired or striven for compulsively, it becomes a monstrous evil and a perpetual justification for the worst forms of tyranny. A realistic despot who is merely interested in personal power and wealth is far less dangerous for humanity than an idealistic tyrant who is possessed and inflated by a glorious vision of Utopia which he or she desperately tries to bring about but which is forever elusive. One can parley with the devil of greed and power (magical pacts with demons have ever been popular), but those possessed by the archetypal gods are beyond human reach. Gods demand sacrifices; they know only how to command, and woe to the leaders of nations whom they have come to possess. Crooked dictators and power-hungry politicians are the small-fry of the nefarious spawn of the ocean of human history; the leaders who are possessed by Utopian visions of power are the sharks of the same bloody and perilous waters. (The reader is referred to Chapter 6 for a detailed treatment of this subject.)

At this point we might introduce the relevance of classical Gnosticism. At the cost of inevitable oversimplification, it may be stated again that among others, there are two important philosophical models of being and reality which continue to have influence in our world—the Platonic and the Gnostic. These views are opposed and contradictory. The Platonic view is attractive but psychologically somewhat flawed. It holds that the ideas existing in the mind of a cosmic Deity can be realized by humans; the world can be made ideal by enlightened philosopher-kings, who know the divine ideas and therefore can implement them. The world is perfectible, says the popularized Platonic view. From this idea, it is but a small step to the concept of Utopia and to the modern socialist, Marxist, fascist, or Islamic dictators, who say that they are in effect the philosopher-kings who know what is true, good and beautiful, and thus have a mandate to remake the world in the image of these Platonic ideas, which they, in their wisdom, have perceived. In contrast is the Gnostic view, which declares that the world is not perfectible. Rather, the world is inherently flawed. According to the Gnostics, this world, this aeon, is dark, but in it there is some light. This light is not to be found in the Platonic ideas, or in the tablets of Moses, but in the souls and spirits of humanity. Utopias, Platonic ideas and ideals are abstractions, which avail us, at best, but very little. The hope of the world is not the Utopian vision of philosopher-kings, but the light that dwells in all human beings. You and I are the hope of the world, and if we are not that, then there is no hope whatsoever.

The Gnostic view declares that the world will never know the true light and, therefore, wholeness or perfection. There can be no earthly Utopia, for the reason that darkness will never know light; only light can know light. Therefore humanity must know itself, and the result of this self-knowledge may not be a perfect world; rather, it will be freedom. The Gnostics held that this internalist position was, in fact, consistent with true Christianity. Did Jesus say, "Make the world perfect," or did he say, "Be ye perfect, even as your father in heaven is perfect"? The father of the world, said the Gnostics, is not the true God, but the true God is indeed the father of humanity. The kingdom of the Saviour, said the Gnostics, is by his own admission not of this world, and he gives us not as the world giveth. Thus the Christianity of Jesus shares in the Gnostic vision.

Individual human beings are the only authentic reality we can contact while living on earth. The state, society, political parties, causes, movements and Utopias are all abstractions. The individual, however, is not an abstraction; the individual is life, the very life of life. The human spirit is the primary reality of life. Said Jung, "If the individual is not truly regenerated in spirit, society cannot be either, for society is the sum total of individuals in need of redemption." As stated above, light must know light, since darkness cannot know light. The ego must know the light of the Self, which is truly the light that shineth in darkness. When such self-knowledge arises, external circumstances begin to slowly modify themselves also. As we individuate, or grow into the stature of our promised fullness, our lives become more meaningful, more rich in content.

As sufficient persons undergo the process of individuation, society and the culture become more meaningful, and more spiritual also. Utopia has not come; indeed, it will never come. What has come, however, is improvement. We cannot perfect this world, but, by improving our consciousness, we can also improve the world. We cannot turn darkness into light, but we can become conscious of ourselves as a small but potent light shining in the darkness. And, above all, we can exercise choice. We can choose consciousness over unconsciousness, freedom over tyranny, intelligence over bovine complacency and mulish rebelliousness. We can choose to know ourselves, and by knowing ourselves, as the Gnostics assured us, we will know the all. And once we have achieved that, why will we need Utopia? Or, perhaps, that will indeed be the true Utopia after all.

7

The Tao of Freedom:
Toward a Voluntary Society

The title of this chapter, "The Tao of Freedom," is meant to be more than an imitation of the popular slogan, which was brought to the attention of the public by such works as Fritjof Capra's *The Tao of Physics*. The Chinese spiritual principle of the Tao lends itself eminently to use as an analogue of a much needed viewpoint within the concerns of the body politic. "Tao" means way: not, as one might initially expect perhaps, a particular way, or specific path to follow, but rather the way or the reality which underlies the action of life and of the soul. The Tao is not a way to which persons and processes must be made to conform, but rather it is simply the way things are. There is, so the ancient Chinese said, an authentic way of being, which is the natural way, not in the sense that it is the way of trees and animals, but in the sense that it is the way that is ordained by the nature of each and every being. If, for example, water is allowed to follow its own course, it will flow as its Tao declares. If the human soul, or psyche, is free of obstacles which stand in the way of its development, it will grow and change according to its own inherent Tao. What makes things, forces and persons malfunction in the world is not so much their contrariness, or their weakness or even evil; rather it is interference with their Tao.

The recognition of this principle of Tao brings with it the maxim of *wu-wei*, often translated as "inaction," but more accurately interpreted as noninterference. Thus the Taoist, one might imagine, would not pose the question, "What shall I do?" but in lieu of it would ask, "What shall I not do; what must I cease to do, so that I may stop interfering with the Tao?" Needless to say, this attitude is not one that rests easily with the Western mind. Inaction, even in the sense of noninterference, is not an acceptable or comfortable notion to most persons in our culture. The idea that is basic to Western humanity's lifestyle is action rather than inaction. If things are bad, or imperfect or unfinished, we want to act, to do something, so that they might change and improve.

Looking at this matter psychologically, we find that the Taoist position, like so many Eastern ideas and ideals, is affinitized to the workings of the unconscious matrix of the human being, while the Western attitude reflects primarily the tendencies and dynamisms of the conscious ego. Jung was aware that the unconscious has its own inbuilt lawfulness, which may be characterized by an abiding inclination toward the amalgamation of more and more unconscious material with consciousness. The Tao of the unconscious impells it to release more and more of itself into consciousness, thereby allowing consciousness to expand and grow at a natural pace. What impedes or stops this growth of consciousness is the presence of factors that interfere with the free entry of unconscious material into the sphere of the conscious ego. Complexes, anxious and fearful attitudes, excessive stress and various tensions are all examples of such interference. The Taoist strives to eliminate such interferences by meditating upon and contemplating nature, as well as by engaging in more intricate exercises (such as the ones described in *The Secret of the Golden Flower*) which reduce interference by bringing about a tranquil condition of mind conducive to what Jung called "the permeability" of the ego to the creative force of the unconscious.

In contradistinction to the ancient Chinese, Westerners value, and frequently overvalue, their conscious ego, and by way of this overvaluation contribute to its alienation from its unconscious background. In extreme cases this may lead to a real loss of the ego's roots within the natural nourishing soil of the unconscious—a "deracination," as Jung called it. In the case of alienation and deracination, the Tao of the unconscious loses its effect upon the ego. The Great Way is lost, and the human personality is left to its own inadequate devices and resources. A curious and paradoxical situation now ensues. The more alienated and deracinated the ego becomes, the more desperately it hangs on to its own notions of self-importance and control. Since the Tao is no longer effective in the individual's life, the personal will and thinking, as well as selfish feelings, enter the arena to make up for the lack of Tao. Doctrinaire beliefs, tyrannical willfulness and personal greed and exploitation take the place of healthy and natural attitudes, and the person's sanity and humanity diminish.

It is obvious then that the course of the alienated ego is a disastrous one. Yet, to a great extent, this has been the course followed by Western humanity both collectively and individually. (Lest we become unfair, it must be recognized that much of Eastern culture, particularly in India, has followed the other extreme of developing little or nothing of the conscious ego, and re-

maining content with a confinement within the unconscious.) For centuries the West has been losing its Tao,
or its soul, as Jung implied in the title of his book
Modern Man in Search of a Soul. Since such phenomena
are never confined to individuals, but affect the totality
of humanity in the culture, the phenomenon of ego-
alienation has had and continues to have its repercus-
sions on the body politic. Alienated psyches produce
alienated cultures and alienated political structures.
Anxious and tyrannical psyches call for anxious and
tyrannical governments which, in emulation of the behavior of the alienated ego, seek to manipulate and control as many facets of life as they possibly can. The
reason for this is quite simple. When humans had access
to the Tao, they could trust the Tao to work out its
designs. All they needed was to cease their interference
with the force of the Tao, and all was taken care of.
When the human being lost touch with the Tao, it had
no one but itself, its personality, its conscious ego to rely
on. In its heart of hearts it knew that its ego was not
equal to the task of total control and responsibility in
life, but it appeared to the human that it had no other
choice. Now, according to the well-known compensatory tendency of the psyche, it began to cover up the
inferiority of its ego with a false feeling of superiority.
Like a frightened person who fights against fear by
whistling in the dark, the deracinated ego puffed itself
up with more and more arrogance, until it came to
assume a position of omnipotence for itself.

The Tao of Government

The implications of this condition within the body
politic are of great interest and relevance. Governments
that functioned within a natural, but largely un-

conscious energy system used power, but only occasionally abused it. Such governments may have been total, but they were not totalitarian. The Tao of their natural openness toward the unconscious imposed natural restraints upon their functioning and made them in fact functionaries of the creative unconscious. The Pharaohs of Egypt, the Emperors of China and Japan, the Incas of Peru and to some degree the Roman Caesars were archetypes in human guise, for which reason they were regarded as divine. The medieval kings and emperors of Europe, while not divine, were rulers by divine right; moreover, they were watched over by the representative of the supreme spiritual archetype, the Pope, called the earthly Vicar of Jesus Christ.

While human frailty and willfulness often upset the applecart of the medieval Tao, on the whole it functioned according to its inherent pattern with considerable efficiency. Only with the coming of the Renaissance, and the subsequent steps in the differentiation of consciousness symbolized by the Protestant Reformation and the Age of Enlightenment, did the dependence of government on the unconscious Tao lessen. Machiavelli's theory of princely power, unrestrained by the Tao of spiritually-based values, was augmented by the rise of the Protestant German princes, particularly the Prussian rulers, and fulfilled by the coming of the absolutist monarchies of Louis XIV, Catherine the Great, and Frederick II of Prussia. The alienated ego was coming into its own. The differentiated human ego now freed itself; increasingly, the ego was emancipated from the former ties to the unconscious. The archaic Tao of religion and its mighty archetypes were no longer effective. Pious individuals still ascended thrones, but the system of government was no longer rooted in the Tao of archaic, yet helpful religious principles. The organic relationship of throne and altar (the yang and yin of medieval government) was severed, and after a few centuries of decline, the thrones fell, their place taken by the alienated structures of secularized republics, periodically replaced by dictatorships.

Today, we still live to a major extent in an age of government without Tao. Here and there the symbolic links with the archetypal structures of the unconscious still remain and give a measure of psychological sustenance to humanity. The queens and kings of England still stand as the archetypal symbols of the soul of their people, their crowned and anointed heads bearing not merely earthly diadems, but the effulgence of a transcendental glory from beyond this world. The Tenno reigns in austere splendor in his vast palace in Tokyo, and as the representative of the Kami deities, performs annual sacrifices and blessings for the fertility and prosperity of the islands of Dai Nippon. But in most portions of the globe, the gods have died, and with them have passed the kings, the earthly representatives of archetypal splendor. The old Tao has departed. As in the China of Confucius, warlords and usurpers march over the countryside and strut in the palaces. The earthly city and the city of God have lost their linkage, and humanity vainly builds towers of Babel to reach heaven once more.

Yet, with these developments, opportunities have arisen which did not exist in the earlier order. Once again the psychological analogy holds true. When the human ego tears itself away from its unconscious background, it has two great options: either it can persist in its alienated arrogance, and thus eventually break down totally or partially; or it may recognize the insufficiency of its present position, turn toward its life-giving background in the unconscious and begin the slow, painful, but ultimately rewarding journey toward authentic selfhood. This journey has been called individuation, because it enhances and completes individuality, allowing the psyche to become an indivisible entity in whom conscious and unconscious are welded together in a state of authentic and final wholeness. How can this picture be applied to the development of state and government?

The Relationship of Citizen and State

Like the human ego, the collective ego of the state has two courses of possible action before it. The state can either become more inflated and bloated with power and a false sense of omnipotence, or it may relinquish much of its power and all of its arrogance and become a fit vehicle for the transformational and growing energies emerging from its constituency. It is an old axiom that in order for God to increase in a person's life, the human self must decrease. We might interpret this statement to mean that if the opportunities and occasions for the growth and individuation of citizens are to increase, the state's power and control must decrease. The totality of the individuals living within the framework of the state are the analogues of the libido, or the energy of the psyche; without them the state is a helpless shell, just as the ego is nothing but a frail shadow without the libidinal force that comes to it from the unconscious recesses.

A great reappraisal of the relationship of citizen and state is necessary in our day, and this reappraisal ought to occur in a way not previously undertaken. To be sure, such a reappraisal has taken place already. It occurred before and during the two great revolutions, the French and the American, and its thrust was primarily philosophical and rational, as indeed one might expect in an age of ego-orientated and differentiated consciousness. There was a spiritual, Hermetic aspect of the Enlightenment also, which has not been completely lost and is still worthy of attention. (See particularly Chapter 9.) Following the philosophical vision of Rousseau and other rationalist philosophers, the thinkers of the Enlightenment formulated the theory of social contract, whereby the citizen enters into a contract or compact with other citizens and thus consents to live in a social organization for specific, practical reasons. The state, therefore, exists for the welfare of its citizens, and it is incumbent upon the latter to be vigilant, lest the state become self-serving and neglectful of its contractual obligations to its citizens. The constitutional monarchy of England and the republic of the United States both can be said to have been greatly influenced by the social contract theory and have benefited by it considerably.

Still, the circumstances which developed over the last two hundred years appear to indicate that the reappraisal of the relationship of citizen and state as carried out by the eighteenth century rationalists was flawed, and that therefore a new reappraisal may indeed be in order. The rationalist theories alluded to had little knowledge of man's spiritual, or as we might call it today, psychological nature. Freedom to the rationalists meant freedom from unreasonable restraints and controls of the citizen's political, economic and social life, on the part of the state. Due to the coincidence in time of these political theories with the Industrial Revolution, the economic aspect of this statement of freedom became most portentous and led to the philosophy of free enterprise which, as even its worst critics admit, led to an era of unprecedented progress and prosperity in all the states where it became operative. While free enterprise built factories, constructed railroads, and gradually, in spite of slums and poverty which it also spawned, created a singularly mobile society embodied in an ever expanding middle class, it left the spiritual resources of humanity virtually untouched. Religion became a Sunday morning diversion without much transformative influence on its practitioners, and the symbols of the dollar bill and the pound sterling became far more meaningful than either the cross or the Bible. A pall of materialism settled on the societies that profited most from the freedom of individual enterprise. It was only a step from this practical materialism to the theoretical materialism of Marx and Engels, which culminated in the political, economic and spiritual tyranny of Lenin, Stalin and Mao Tse-tung. But while millions of sincere and idealistic persons over the last three-quarters of a century, often in disregard of the Marxist hecatombs of the Gulag, of China, of Cambodia and other places, flocked to the banner of Marxism, declaring the system of free enterprise and with it the social contract state bankrupt, not many recognized that this bankruptcy might be remedied by a reappraisal of the social contract system in psychological terms.

Today an ever increasing number have begun to recognize that it is nothing less than rank folly to abandon a system which has been predominantly successful and only partially unsuccessful and exchange it for a model of government that has proven itself to be a cruel, vicious failure in all human terms, and ultimately gave up the ghost because of its inability to survive economically. Assuredly, it would be far more reasonable and useful to reappraise the raison d'être of the social contract state—with its various freedoms, including that of enterprise—and, moreover, to conduct such a reappraisal in terms of the spiritual needs of the human soul or psyche within a contemporary, yet timeless context. The remaining portion of our discourse, therefore, shall be devoted to the essentials of such a reappraisal.

The Social Contract State

The social contract state is one of the most promising philosophies of government ever to emerge in the known history of humankind. Its usefulness exists not chiefly in the economic sphere, as previously envisioned by those whose vision seldom extends beyond their bank balance, but rather in the sphere of the realization of the spiritual transformative potential that resides in the human being. At one time, in the days of the divine kings of ancient days, and later in the centuries of the alliance of throne and altar, the state itself possessed archetypal or symbolic power. With the coming of higher forms of differentiated consciousness, this Tao of archetypal potential passed to humanity at large. In our age the state can no longer save the human being, any more than a distant saviour in ancient Palestine could do so. Men and women must save themselves, for in Jung's words, they and they alone are the carriers of consciousness. In our day the state must be a framework, a convenience for the benefit of the individual consciousness of its citizens. It is easy to see that the primary requisite of a convenience is that it be convenient. It is equally easy to see that most modern governments are not convenient, at least not for the purposes indicated. Governments almost as a matter of course assume that they are called to control the lives of their citizens, that the circumstance of a particular group of leaders having risen to their positions entitles them to regulate, control and interfere with the lives and activities of the governed. As if the scrap of paper declaring a person to be such-and-such an official in a government would make a god of him or her, bestowing superhuman powers of wisdom and insight. Such assumptions were perhaps in order in archaic times, when rulers were gods, but they are assuredly out of place in our day. When we were children, we spoke as children and, we might say, we obeyed like children. To transpose the values and attitudes of the childhood of consciousness into its age of maturity, or even into its period of adolescence, is a grave mistake.

Authoritarian governments, whether established by votes or by bayonets, are not different from parents who forget that their offspring are no longer living in the childhood of the human race. Authoritarian statesmen forget that what was acceptable in the days of the pharaohs is no longer useful or even morally permissible in our times and in our culture. In contrast to the authoritarian position, however, is another, which while seldom mentioned, nevertheless has much merit. It has sometimes been called the "libertarian" position, although other names could be given to it also. (The references here and elsewhere in the present book to "libertarian" have no connection to the political party of that name.) One of the most simple and yet supremely convincing formulations of the libertarian position is contained in a proposed statement by a hypothetical libertarian candidate in James C. Ingebretsen's *A Libertarian Catechism*. The candidate addresses the citizen as follows:

> You as a person are better able to control your life than I am. Your life is your personal affair, for better or for worse, except as in the living of your life you may impair

or endanger the life and livelihood of others. No person nor set of persons on this earth has any logical right to interfere with you except as you may do injury to them.

The argument presented here is little short of irrefutable. What right could anyone claim legitimately with respect to another beyond the defense of himself or herself? If we as individuals do not possess such a right, why should we delegate it to an entity of convenience, such as the agency of the state? In practice this means that government should be in the main limited to the defense of life and property; it should not be a guardian of morals, a regulator of private or even public behavior, unless this behavior is directly and demonstrably harmful to the welfare of some citizen or citizens. Neither should government be a distributor or redistributor of wealth, a restrictor of freedom in the marketplace where goods and services are exchanged. A government that arrogates the right unto itself to manipulate and regulate the behavior of its citizens morally, politically, educationally, socially, financially or economically is clearly out of bounds.

In terms of psychological principles, this means that government should respect the Tao of freedom. Human beings are not on earth to be citizens, or taxpayers or socially engineered pawns of other human beings; rather they are here in order to grow, to transform, to become their authentic selves. Whether a government forces a woman by law to carry a fetus to full maturity without recourse to an abortion, or whether it confiscates another's justly earned profits by taxation or expropriation, it does psychological injury to the sovereignty and integrity of persons. It matters little whether in so doing the government is motivated by archaic theological notions of the precise beginnings of human life, or by medieval notions of a Robin Hood-like welfare state.

The consistent need for the curbing of governmental power must be seen as a psychological necessity, advancing the individuation of the psyche. What is needed above all is consistency in the universal application of freedom. It is psychologically inconsistent for a state to guarantee women's rights but not the rights of wage earners and entrepreneurs to retain the fruits of their labors. It is equally untenable to demand freedom of religious worship and conscience and at the same time to regulate by law the most private sexual behavior and preferences of persons. The key word in the entire field of libertarian versus authoritarian values is *choice*. Unconscious humanity was capable of few choices. The growth of consciousness, however, both depends on and manifests in the making of choices. We individuate not by fiat, but by trial and error; not by being good, but by being free. The state or government must not only permit, but encourage this choice-making function of the human psyche, for by so doing it advances the growth of consciousness. Jung has taught us that spiritual growth, expansion of consciousness is hard, that it entails difficulties, darkness and suffering, along with ecstasies, joys and splendid vistas of light. It stands to reason that this condition, characteristic of the individuating ego must also apply to a society in which individuation takes place. The state has to cease to envision that it can make itself into an ideal society without want, sorrow and failure. Instead of pursuing such notions, state, government and society must address itself to creating and guarding opportunities for choice. Where there is choice, there is growth, love, creativity. Where choice is absent, even though there is equality, prosperity, physical health and well-being, there will be minimal growth, atrophied love and the vanishing of creativity.

The Great Tao, said the Chinese, is without form, yet it governs the movements of all things. Specific forms come and go, but the vital surge of the Tao remains. The forms only matter to the degree that they permit the Tao to come forth and accomplish its never-ending work of transformation. Democracies, tyrannies, capitalism, socialism, feudalism, syndicalism, fascism: all are forms and structures that rise and vanish like a dream. God is not a capitalist or a socialist, a democrat or a fascist; God is the Tao, the Way leading to movement, growth, consciousness and choice.

Through a thousand forms, by way of myriad structures, God, the Tao, the Pleroma seeks its own level of ineffable greatness. It cares little for politicians, presidents and dictators; it cares only for consciousness. Mortals of human frame can do one of two things: either they can resist, or they can accept the Tao. Authoritarian government, like an alienated, arrogant human ego, is a resister. A truly freedom-oriented government, if it were ever to exist, would be the accepter, the choice creator, the facilitator of consciousness. Without coercive manipulation of persons or circumstances, without special privileges accorded from the seat of power, with faith and confidence in the human potential for consciousness, such government would offer and guarantee only one gift, one boon, one promise: namely, choice—the choice of freedom, which is Tao.

8

Shamanic America:
Ancient Foundations of
American Culture

It has been said poetically that no man is an island. Self-knowledge, individuation—these modern expressions of Gnosis are not accomplished in a vacuum, but in a cultural and social context. Such a context inevitably possesses its own geographical, ethnic and historical roots, without which both the process of individuation and its psychological features become incomprehensible. In spite of much talk heard today about global or planetary spirituality, it is important to recognize that neither spirituality nor self-knowledge can begin on a global scale but rather must originate and be nourished within a specific cultural context. We must also recognize that the best insurance against incursions into our lives by the malefic aspect of the unconscious is delineating parameters and establishing specific contexts for our concerns. The unconscious has an oceanic quality and, like the ocean, possesses titanic energy, but for its energy to act in a constructive manner, it must move within certain parameters.

It is important to keep in mind that the context of our

143

culture is important for us, and that it has an essential bearing on our psychic processes. We do not live and move and have our being solely in our own isolated egoic backyard, nor do we live in the vastness of the entire planet. We each have a culture, a history and a contextual milieu within which our own alchemy operates. In the language of alchemy, we might say that our culture is the retort within which our transformation takes place. Thus it is incumbent upon us to inquire insightfully into the nature and character of this retort and thereby contribute to the advancement of our transformation.

American culture did not begin when Columbus arrived on the continent. As the child is father to the man, so the ancient America of the original inhabitants represents the ancestral foundations of the culture, upon which the structure erected later rests. One of the most remarkable developments of recent decades has been the growing interest evinced by many people in our culture in Native Americans, previously often called American Indians. Applying psychological terms to the cultural context, one might say that Native Americans have been for a long time the principal carriers of the shadow of white civilization in many countries on the American continents. The concept of the shadow is by now so well known that it seems unnecessary to explain it at length. It may be sufficient to state that in depth psychology the shadow is a rejected part of the individual psyche which nevertheless remains attached to the ego as a shadow remains attached to a physical object. The shadow contains the ambivalent or undesirable elements of the psyche which have been permitted to drop into the shadowland of the unconscious. Until this shadow is brought to the surface of conscious awareness, it remains a haunting, malefic presence within the human soul.

It is likely that, at least in the United States, the shadow of the ancient inhabitant, the Native American, is coming to conscious awareness at this time to advance the individuation of the collective psyche. It is useful to note that in Europe where exposure to Native American culture was nonexistent, and where people were fond of reading romantic literature about the "noble savages" of the Old West, fictional Apache and Mohican warriors were the subject of only positive projections. C. G. Jung himself was fond of those elements of ancient America which he had an opportunity to contact. His noted encounter and long friendship with a chief of the Pueblo Indians of New Mexico is well known. Another interesting incident is recounted by Jung's disciple, Marie-Louise von Franz. In her journals she recorded the following conversation:

> When I once remarked to Jung that his psychological insights and his attitude to the unconscious seemed to me in many respects the same as those of the most archaic religions, for example Shamanism, or the religion of the Naskapi Indians who have neither priest nor ritual but who merely follow their dreams which they believe are sent by the "immortal great man in the heart," Jung answered with a laugh: "Well, that's nothing to be ashamed of. It is an honor!"

Like C. G. Jung and other Europeans, most adults now living in the United States have had no contact with people who were part of the past great conflict between Native and white Americans. Could they converse with their great-grandparents, they might hear a few unpleasant tales of wagon trains attacked on their westward treks, or of men, women and children slaughtered, farmhouses burned, women raped and children abducted. Only a few decades ago, many elderly people could recount such events. Shadow projections in this area did not occur without cause. Not so long ago the conflict between American cultures was fierce, cruel and productive of much pain and anger on both sides. It may be useful to keep in mind that these memories, along with Wounded Knee and other atrocities committed by whites, are also part of the psychic residue of the sorrowful and violent course of American history.

It was not only the bloody conflict between Native Americans and white settlers, but also some of the customs and religious practices of the native cultures that horrified European settlers and created mighty shadows in the collective American psyche. When the Spaniard Bernardo Diaz wrote of his first encounter with the sacrificial altars of the Aztec empire of Montezuma in his work *The Conquest of New Spain,* Europeans could not help but be revolted by the descriptions of the chambers of the gods covered from floor to ceiling with the blood of human sacrifices, the buildings themselves reeking with the stench of human blood. While it has been noted that history is always written by the victors and embodies their point of view, there is no denying the veracity of reports of thousands of human sacrifices carried out by the Aztecs and some other native cultures at the time of the Spanish conquest. Since many of the sacrificial victims were abducted from the ranks of other nations, it is easy to see that these practices carried overtones of genocide. At a time when the celebrations of Christopher Columbus's jubilee are marred by accusations of genocide in connection with the activities of the Genoese admiral of Spain, these considerations may help to establish a needed perspective.

Consciousness does not increase with one-sided vision. Even as the view of many nineteenth century Americans was unduly prejudiced against the native population of the land, so the unbalanced apologies of the present era evidence a different kind of one-sidedness. In spite of the optimism rampant in the psyches of many people in the United States, the relatively brief history of this country, like any other national history, is filled with sorrow, cruelty and conflict. Deep wounds fester in the collective soul which will not be healed by faultfinding. (For example, one may also mention the abiding trauma of the Civil War, the fratricidal horror of which still haunts the nation.) The purpose of the present analysis is not to adopt a one-sided position of advocating the values of ancient America, but rather to advance a conscious understanding of the ways in which the shamanic culture of the original inhabitants became a part of the psychic atmosphere of the present culture and how it may continue to influence developments from here on.

Native Americans have become the symbol of the archaic, buried self, the ancient and therefore mostly ambivalent part of our cultural heritage. The repression of the spirit of the Native American was great; indeed, it was greater than the repression of the spirit of the dark-skinned Africans forcibly transplanted from their native Africa to America. The implications of this wounding at the collective psychological level are significant. In this era of *Bury My Heart at Wounded Knee* and of the increased interest in Native American spirituality and shamanism, there is a danger of sentimentality rooted in guilt feelings about past injustices and an adolescent nostalgia for conditions experienced only in the imagination. The insecure ego reacts to the pressures of an uncomfortable shadow in the uncon-

scious sometimes by hostility and at other times by
maudlin sentimentality. One response is as counterproductive as the other.

Yet the current sympathy for the Native American is
important because it indicates an emergence, or at least
an attempted emergence, of the suppressed, enshad-
owed side of the unconscious of our culture. The darkness must be brought into light, and the hidden must be
revealed; only then can the soul be whole. Native Americans are not strangers but maltreated and neglected
relatives in the household of American culture. They
are not savage aliens, but noble old neighbors whom we
first fought with, then persecuted and finally forgot. In
spite of their physical inconspicuousness and numerical
diminishment, these noble old neighbors have much to
contribute to the body cultural and to the community of
mind and spirit. A few hundred years is not a long time
in the world of archetypes, and often the old symbols of
the archaic unconscious are the truly potent and persis-
tent ones.

Symbolic reality is a strange and savage land, in
which old images live with a fierce vitality, while more
recent emblems and signs fade into insignificance.
Could it be that the feathered totems and solemn peace
pipes may prove more powerful in the end than the star-
spangled banner? And, while the proud American her-
aldic eagle wearies in his flight, might not the thunder-
bird and the majestic plumed serpent Quetzalcoatl rise
in some renewed shape on archetypal wings? The archetypes of ancient America are not dead, and time and
again they may awaken from their aeonial rest to contribute their symbolic wisdom and vitality to the falter-
ing structures of our culture. If our attitude toward
them is devoid of repression on the one hand, and of
immature, sentimental romanticization on the other,

then these archetypes may still act as messengers of wholeness, emissaries of the truths of the soul for us in our day.

The Quetzalcoatl Archetype

A few examples of archetypal motifs may illustrate the nature of this task of psycho-spiritual assimilation. (The reader is referred for more information to reputable sources of archaic American tales, such as *Primitive Mythologies* by Joseph Campbell, in his series *The Masks of God.* I would caution readers to consult reputable works written by scholars of cultural anthropology, mythology and religion rather than the trendy but superficial literature abounding at present.)

The pre-Columbian cultures of Central and South America have many important myths which contain useful and salvific secrets for contemporary people. In many respects, these cultures were amazingly complex and sophisticated, although they were curiously lacking in technological and psychological refinement. (Thus, for example, the Inca culture did not possess the wheel and had no written language, with the exception of knotted strings.) From these cultures came one of the greatest indigenous archetypes, the hero-god Quetzalcoatl, who originated somewhere in Central Mexico, but who later became an almost universal deity of Central and parts of South America. The names given this hero-god varied, but the essential features remained the same, for his names in the various languages all meant "feathered (or winged) serpent."

Most legends, documents and monuments show Quetzalcoatl in human form. Thus he was human, serpentine and birdlike at once. To the student of mythology, this combination is quite significant.

Human beings are often taken to represent the dual principles of earth and fire (the body being earthly, while the indwelling life or soul is envisioned as heavenly fire). The serpent, being amphibious, stands as a water symbol, and the bird as a symbol of air. The four elements together in one being add up to a complete tetramorph, a fourfold image of wholeness. This symbolism alone identifies Quetzalcoatl as a representational paradigm of the individuated ego, the deified human, similar to the archetype of Christ, which Jung related to the central archetype of the psyche, the Self. Jung has often stated that the savior figures of various religions, including Christianity, were symbolic of the archetype of wholeness, known as the Self.

Like Jesus, Quetzalcoatl was the son of the universal father and of a virgin, and one of his most solemn titles was "he who was born of the virgin." Spanish priests, who eventually became the chief chroniclers of what remained of the ancient religion, recorded many strange stories about Quetzalcoatl. One wrote that he was a white man who came from the north, with a strong forehead, long nose, big eyes and a flowing beard. He had a mitre on his head, wore a long white robe ornamented with small crosses and bore a sickle in his hand. Another wrote that Quetzalcoatl was instrumental in introducing metal smelting, the cutting of gems and the forging of metal objects. These strange descriptions suggest that Quetzalcoatl can be identified as a bishop, hierophant and an alchemist, who, by the power of the sacred fire, can break down the gross ore of physical nature and bring forth beautiful and useful objects. (Mircea Eliade in his work on alchemy identifies the ancient blacksmiths as the first alchemists.) As a hierophant wearing a mitre on his head, Quetzalcoatl also seems to have been a priestly alchemist who changes bread and wine into the flesh and blood of divinity.

Characteristically, Quetzalcoatl is also said to have taught the people that corn was edible and stained certain fruits with his blood. According to the ancient calendar, Quetzalcoatl was born on the day of the Seven Canes and died on the day of the One Cane. This curious fact may symbolize reducing the seven to the one, or reestablishing unity from the sevenfold system of differentiation. Esoteric teachings frequently divide the human being into seven components, which are in need of integration. (For details of the Quetzalcoatl myth, see Joseph Campbell, as well as James M. Pryse, quoted in Manly Palmer Hall, *The Secret Teachings of All Ages*.)

As a serpent, Quetzalcoatl bathed in the Xicapaya spring and built mighty subterranean labyrinths and grottoes where he dwelt for extended periods. In memory of this, many temples devoted to his worship had elaborate underground chambers, which according to reports, served as halls of initiation. He was also a great sorcerer, a great necromancer. He worked miracles and entrusted his miraculous powers to successors. (Initiators usually establish an "apostolic" succession of some sort, as the universal testimony of many diverse cultures reveals.) Quetzalcoatl is also credited with the invention of the hieroglyphic methods of writing and was the master of language. The qualities of the archetypal hierophant are quite apparent in these details. To speak and write means to articulate the unconscious, to bring content from the dark regions of the mind into consciousness. One who cannot speak is less than human, while one who speaks beautifully and meaningfully is more than human. Thus verbal communication is a divine act.

As in most hero-myths, Quetzalcoatl also had an adversary, known as Tetzatlipoca, lord of darkness and nocturnal sorcery. Tetzatlipoca decided that to rid him-

self of Quetzalcoatl he would poison him. Treacher-
ously, Quetzalcoatl is administered a slow-acting
poison. When he recognizes that he is dying, Quetzalcoatl leaves his sacred place in Tulla, orders his dwelling to be burnt and travels to the sea to depart. The
details of his death are the most enchanting parts of the
entire myth. Accompanied by musicians, young men
and maidens, all of whom bear flowers, Quetzalcoatl
journeys to Cholula, where he lingers for some time
while the poison works and he slowly sickens. As the
hour of his death approaches, he blesses four young men
who have accompanied him and sends them home, en-
trusting to them his mysteries, and bidding them to
await his return in the future.

The legends vary concerning Quetzalcoatl's final departure. According to one version, he travels to the sea
near Vera Cruz. At the seashore, he calls out to the
ocean with a thunderous voice. Out of the waves
emerges a magic raft composed of the bodies of ser-
pents. Quetzalcoatl steps into this boat of living rep-
tiles, which swiftly carries him off in an eastward direction, the direction from which he came to the western
continent aeons before. According to another version,
Quetzalcoatl removes his feathered clothing and serpent mask and sets himself on fire. Out of the embers of
his funeral pyre arise luminous birds that fly to the four
directions, while his unburnt heart flies up into the air
and becomes the morning star.

The Quetzalcoatl legend has certain similarities to
the story of Dionysus who also journeys to the sea with
ecstatic maidens and youths and disappears. What does
all this mean? Who is this mysterious hierophant, who
is at once man, snake and bird? Where did he come
from; where did he go; when and how will he return?
Speculations and theories are many, but they are of lit-

tle use. Some say that Quetzalcoatl was the star-spawned offspring of space, an adept traveler among the galaxies, who may come back from the sky someday on a fiery chariot. Others say that he came from mysterious and doomed Atlantis, from the land that sank under the waves, and that he brought magic and divine light from the sunken continent to the utter-most West. But are not the stars also within us, and is not the heaven of the soul vast enough to account for the mystery of Quetzalcoatl? Moreover, is there not also present within us a vast archetypal continent, sunk under the waves of the unconscious, in the depths where King Neptune and the sea nymphs dwell? That vast, inward, hidden Atlantis is certainly large enough to serve as the homeland of great Quetzalcoatl and to receive him again when he departs from mortal shores.

One thing is certain: in the story of Quetzalcoatl, a great messianic and hierophantic myth has been bequeathed to us. In it we can recognize elements reminiscent of Christ, Hermes, Dionysus, Osiris and other hero-gods. The profundity of this myth is great, and its archetypal power vast. Many have found inspiration in this story of divine exile, and many may be guided by it still. Ancient America has given to us a myth of such sublime archetypal nature that it may well compare with the greatest myths of Greece, Egypt and the Celtic lands.

The Trickster, a Plains Archetype

While the mighty empires of the Maya, the Aztec, Quiche, Inca and other cultures of Mexico, Central and South America left us much highly refined mythological and religious lore, the same cannot be said of the tribes inhabiting the great plains of North America. For centuries these people roamed the prairies. Poor and without a highly developed technology, they often struggled to survive. In the latter part of the eighteenth century, they briefly achieved a measure of material and cultured wealth and power, as the result of a new, powerful ally, the horse. The Spanish conquerors of Mexico had imported the common European horse to the New World. Some of these horses ran wild, and their offspring congregated in large herds of mustangs which then migrated northward. From these herds of mustangs, the Plains people domesticated riding horses. Mounted on horses, the Plains natives became fierce warriors and skilled buffalo hunters, rulers of the prairie. Mobility, the time-honored Hermetic quality of consciousness, had become a great stimulator of psychological and cultural forces among these people. Thus the short-lived glory of the mounted hunters and warriors can be attributed to the mobility brought to them by the horse, even as so much of the power and glory of our current civilization is attributable to the horsepower of the combustion engine. (One wonders whether this glory also will be short-lived.)

While the Maya, Aztec and related legends raise many curious questions, and many farfetched and speculative notions, no one of sound mind could attribute the legends and customs of the Comanche, the Cheyenne, the Pawnee, the Sioux and the Blackfoot to mysterious Atlantis, or to the metamorphosed teachings of Buddhist missionaries from Asia. These native peoples were almost without exception true representatives of the archaic, primeval human psyche, as close to the mysterious, unconscious source of human life as they were to the earth and the sun.

The gods of the Plains peoples were rarely organized into a structured pantheon. Gods and spirits were rather a vague grouping of powers, seldom ranked as lesser or greater, and not always possessing specifically defined attributes or cosmic roles. As the archetypes of the collective unconscious may be said to gradually define themselves to the young and developing human ego, so too the gods of archaic humanity are still largely without a hierarchy, without specialized offices and provinces of dominion. It may be useful to remember that this description of the typical spiritual beliefs of ancient peoples is not meant to be a denigration of them and the culture they developed. Increasing differentiation of spiritual systems brings with it a corresponding loss of true numinosity. Well-defined categories of supernal beings tend to render them less, not more divine. The more people know *about* God, the less they know *of* God. Archaic spirituality is in many ways closer to the source, closer to the original divine ground of being than its more differentiated successor. Once a high degree of psychological differentiation has taken place, it is nearly impossible to recapture the primal vision available to the less differentiated consciousness. Thus it may be exceedingly difficult for members of today's culture to recreate the kind of simple, uncomplicated spirituality found among the surviving remnants of early cultures, such as the Siberian tribes, the Aboriginals of Australia and certain Native American peoples. While the two paths thus diverge, contemporary Americans can still learn a great deal by contemplating various features of archaic American spirituality and adapting it to current cultural and psychological needs. Such adaptation and assimilation, however, require a firm grounding in contemporary cultural archetypes as well as a firm, disciplined ego structure.

One of the more important and potentially useful archetypal figures of the native peoples of North America is the trickster. The trickster spirit, particularly popular in the lore of the Blackfoot people, is a divine spirit, usually disguised in a temporary animal form. Animal gods appear frequently in Native American myths, and they usually symbolize archetypal powers in disguise for a specific purpose. The trickster is a strange composite of hero, defender of the weak, punisher of evildoers and worker of farcical mischief and weird practical jokes. The trickster goes by many names among the various nations and tribes: in the Pacific Northwest, he is the Raven; the Pawnee identify him as Coyote; while the Blackfoot name for him translates as Spider. The myths of the trickster show him at times to be the creator of the world and of humankind. In these instances, he brings about the origin of some natural phenomena by way of a trick or playful accident. Even the world itself is created as the byproduct of some piece of mischief. Often the joke is on people or on various creatures, but at times on the trickster himself. Trickster figures of various kinds appear in African tales (one of these is a rabbit, the prototype of the Br'er Rabbit stories told by African slaves in America), while in Europe the trickster appears as Reinecke, as Raynard the Fox, and also as Bluejay. However, the archetypal figure of the trickster has been most clearly and impressively expressed by the native peoples of North America.

In his work *On the Psychology of the Trickster Archetype*, C. G. Jung connects the trickster with the shadow. Both trickster and shadow help the psyche move toward greater meaning. Eventually both the shadow and the trickster change into their opposites; instead of being disturbing and menacing elements that threaten consciousness, they become the helpers and redeemers of the ego. Jung's insights are reinforced by the fact that many wise people have been known to have an element of the trickster in their psychological makeup; indeed they often acted as tricksters themselves. H. P. Blavatsky, Gurdjieff, and earlier St. Albertus Magnus and St. Theresa of Avila all manifested humorous, trickster-like qualities. Alan Watts often mentioned the ancient belief that God himself is a trickster, eternally playing hide-and-seek with himself. Omnipotence, said Watts, implies the power of self-restriction, and self-restriction in turn includes self-deception. The wisdom of the archaic proto-psychology of ancient peoples can thus bring an ancient truth back into our consciousness once more. As represented by the lore of the Plains peoples, the trickster carries an extremely important message. As a symbol of anarchy, disorder, lawlessness and defiance of authority, the trickster can be a disquieting or menacing figure to civilized society.

In his work, *Archetypes of the Collective Unconscious*, Jung says: "Anyone who belongs to a sphere of culture that seeks the perfect state somewhere in the past must feel very queerly indeed when confronted by the figure of the trickster. He is a forerunner of the savior, and, like him, God, man and animal at once. He is both subhuman and superhuman, a bestial and divine being, whose chief and most alarming characteristic is his unconsciousness." American culture needs to discover the repressed archetype of the trickster. The dour and solemn tone of Calvinism, a religious orientation which has been all too influential in the shaping and maintaining of American culture (See Chapter 9), makes no allowances for the figure of the trickster. Yet, without this archetype, how can there be effective freedom? Freedom entails the ability to be playful, mischievous and even irresponsible. Artists, prophets and creative persons of all sorts most frequently function outside of the rigid parameters and stifling conformity of societal roles and rules, of an arbitrarily defined norm of useful pursuits and a work ethic based on the same. Rediscovering the trickster's spirit of play could help us revive our culture artistically and creatively, to say nothing of stimulating its spiritual dimension. Archetypes like the trickster, drawn from the mythic framework of the Native Americans, are certainly worthy of our serious attention.

Induced Ecstasy

Another element of the Native American spiritual heritage, which has received scant attention until recent times, is alteration of consciousness by means of ecstasy inducing practices. The communion of native shamans with the spiritual world most frequently involved trance, ecstasy, drumming, dance and the ingestion of psychotropic substances which joined the shaman to the world of the spirits or gods. To white Americans who regarded sitting in church and listening to lengthy sermons as the essence of true religion, the idea of initiatory spirituality based on the altering of consciousness probably seemed frightening and alien. However, according to the Gnostic Gospels, the Christian religion itself was once a mystery religion with an initiatory structure, in which various means were employed that altered consciousness. (The same can be asserted of ancient Hinduism and Zoroastrianism, with their *Soma* and *Haoma* drinks.) Initiation and the altering of consciousness, whether through ingested substances, yogic exercises, breath control, or other means, seems to have been the universal practice of effective religious life in certain periods of history. That at least some of these features enriched religion greatly, and that their loss represents a loss for the culture itself has been recognized by many scholars. Mircea Eliade, for example, said that one of the characteristics of the modern world is the disappearance of any meaningful rites of initiation. Many effective tools of initiation have also disappeared.

Various plant substances were used traditionally by Native Americans to induce an exalted or receptive state of mind in which the mysteries of the spiritual worlds might be received and appreciated. One of the most important of these plants, which in a purely secular way has found entry into white society is, of course, tobacco. All native groups south of the Great Lakes cultivated tobacco, and regarded this plant as a way of making contact with the Great Spirit. The smoke of the tobacco plant, like the fumes of the ancient Hebrew altar of burnt offerings, ascended bearing prayers and wishes from people on earth. The same substance was used in conferences to bring about a state of serious and pacific intent, so that discussions could proceed without anger and anxiety. Splendid myths describe the divine-human origins of the tobacco plant and its use.

The mystic uses of the tobacco plant were many, not the least of which was as an opener of the door to dreams. It was believed that if a person smoked before going to sleep, the dreams received under the inspiration of tobacco would be significant and easily recalled. It is interesting to note that the two leading exponents of modern dream interpretation, Freud and Jung, were both devoted to smoking tobacco, and that their dreams were instrumental in opening up a new field of psychology. Perhaps this curious fact tends to prove that when put to sacred use, consciousness altering substances can still work their magic, while the same substances, put to trivial or secular use, not only lose their sacred effect, but can become destructive. This principle may be applied to the use of many substances. For example, alcohol, a sacred substance in Judaism and Christianity, has caused much mischief when divorced from its sacred context.

Other consciousness altering practices were used among the native peoples of the American continent. Dancing, drumming, sweat lodges, inhaling not only tobacco, but also wood smoke, along with inhaling or ingesting many varieties of plants, herbs and fungi were all utilized in this manner. A prominent and, in one instance, tragic example of such practices was the famous ghost dance initiated by the prophet Wovoka, who received a divine revelation of a special dance to give to his people. The form and rhythm of this dance were unique. As its name indicates, the dance had spiritistic overtones; it was believed that the dance would bring back large numbers of Indian dead and revive the old glories of Indian life, while the "white man" would disappear from the earth. The famous Sioux chief Sitting Bull, who was an enthusiastic ghost dancer, was killed by army troups right after he presided over a dance.

The importance of ecstatic spirituality has been woefully neglected in modern American society. The reemergence of psychedelic substances and their frequent use for spiritual purposes in and since the 1960s and 1970s highlights this need. If such needs are not addressed wisely and insightfully in the daylight of research, they will thrive in distorted ways in the night of illegality and counterculture rebelliousness.

The Influence of Shamanic America

The foregoing account makes clear that there are many distinctive features of ancient or shamanic America, which have deeply affected the white majority culture that supplanted it. In his travels in the United States, Jung formed the opinion that the psychic influence of the native culture is still considerable. Though little outer evidence of the presence of the native peoples remains, in a mysterious, secret way, the old archetypes and psychic patterns continue to stimulate our culture.

An example of this stimulation is the fact that American democratic institutions owe more to the Native American than to any European institutional framework. While the Hermetic spirituality in the ideology of the Enlightenment may be said to have been the psychological motivator of the founders of the American Republic, Native American institutions served as the model for putting such ideals into practice. The Iroquois Federation uniting the tribal nations of the northeast gave the American founders a structure for joining the colonies into a federated national system. Thomas Jefferson, Benjamin Franklin and George Washington all befriended Indians and learned much from their thinking. A good case may be made for the theory that as long as the esoteric and Hermetic spirit of the founders of the Republic remained influential, the appreciation and influence of the native peoples continued. The cruel and rapacious treatment accorded to them at a later time came from a cultural current very different from the one embraced by the founders. (The reader is referred to an excellent study of this subject by anthropologist Jack Weatherford, called *Indian Givers: How the Indians of the Americas Transformed the World.*)

The continuing existence of the shamanistic stream in the American psyche is also borne out by numerous historical currents and events in our history. One example is the strong individualism carried in our collective psyche. The native peoples of North America, though tribal in organization, were oriented to a kind of individualism. Even more was this the case with the shamans among them. According to the best known authority on the subject, Mircea Eliade, shamans are individual heroes of consciousness and technicians of ecstasy. The depths of the American psyche harbor at least as much of the hunter shaman as they do of the Yankee pioneer and trader. The great collectivist ideologies of this century, including anarchism, Marxist socialism and communism, were always alien to the psyche of the American people. Such currents were invariably importations from Europe and flourished primarily among recent immigrants. The worth and power of the individual was always the underlying foundation of the thinking of the people in this land, and this foundation may be closely related to the hidden, yet potent influence of our archaic psychological foundations.

Another powerful shamanic tendency that is expressed repeatedly in our culture might be called the spiritistic-ecstatic phenomenon. Initially embodied in early charismatic religious expressions, such as the Shakers, speakers-in-tongues and revivalists, the great Spiritualist movement of the mid-nineteenth century became the principal embodiment of shamanism in the mainstream culture. Speaking with spirits of the invisible world, often through the agency of entranced mediums, is certainly a phenomenon of classical shamanism in all parts of the world. This phenomenon continues to manifest in the form of the many reports of communications with spaceships during the 1950s, as well as in the channeling fad of the 1970s and 1980s. As noted, the psychedelic revolution of the 1960s also owes much of its inspiration to ancient shamanism. In spite of its excesses, this era unleashed a great creative and psychospiritual fervor in the culture, which in certain ways has not yet abated.

All of these currents have one thing in common: though they are genuinely related to shamanism, they lack the safeguards and controls of tradition which they possessed in ancient societies. The responsibility for the success or failure of such activities, then, rests strictly with the individual practitioner. This circumstance brings dangers when the practitioner possesses little psychological development.

Finally, our shamanic heritage has also found expression in the earth-centered spirituality of recent years. Devotees of Gaia, of Goddess worship and other ideological advocates of ecology and conservation all claim the Native American as their model. As is the case with so many trendy developments, this movement also needs careful scrutiny and evaluation. There is no doubt that the Native Americans respected the earth and possessed a mythological basis for so doing. By the same token, it must be remembered that this respect never assumed the unbalanced form it tends to have among such contemporary enthusiasts. The predominant term used among Native Americans for the earth is "mother," but this term does not carry the implications of "mother earth," used among non-native people pursuing the new chthonocentric trends. In addition, one must recall that the sun is always represented in native lore as "father" and is regarded as equal with earth. (Jung's friend among the Pueblo people considered it his duty to make "our father sun" rise every morning.) On the whole, there is minimal warrant for claiming the Native American as the prototype for some sort of matriarchal earth worship with eclectic overtones.

What then of the worship of earth, with or without Native American associations? How beautiful such phrases as "our oneness with mother earth"! They make us think of fertile fields, lush forests and rushing rivers. Yet there is danger too in such immersion in earth. We are a culture largely alienated from earth. As the result of our mastery over this element, we have lost touch with it. Because of our very isolation from earth and nature, we have come to sentimentalize it, to fill it with psychological projections which are often inappropriate. Thus we fail to see the dark side of nature, the terrifying aspects of earth, the capricious, cruel and enslaving aspects of the beautiful yet hazardous realities of life on the planet. Yes, we live on this earth; yes, we have to behave with a sense of responsibility toward it and toward the natural matrix within which we exist. It is an unwise bird that befouls its own nest. But we must not forget that the nest is not the same as the bird. The exoteric and esoteric traditions declare that earth is not the only home for human beings, that we did not grow like weeds from the soil. While our bodies indeed may have originated on this earth, our inner essence did not. To think otherwise puts us outside of all of the known spiritual traditions and separates us from the wisdom of the seers and sages of every age. Though wise in their own ways, Native Americans have small connection with this rich spiritual heritage.

Ancient America, shamanic America, is very much with us, and it still has much to teach us, although its teachings may differ from the content our projections place on them. Now that these teachings have ceased to hold our shadow, we must examine them with consciousness. We owe this to ourselves and to the spirit of our cultural ancestors.

9

Hermetic and Puritan America:
Opposites in Our Society

The contemporary social arena of the United States is characterized by a cacophony of competing voices, all claiming to be the authentic, the true voice of this country. On the left of the socio-political spectrum, many voices are heavily colored by late nineteenth and early twentieth century European thought. I am referring here primarily to the dialectical materialism of Marx and Engels in its several variants, some amplified by Lenin. Born of the conditions of nineteenth century western Europe and championed by impoverished, restive intellectual immigrants to the United States from various European countries, Marxist thought has become well-nigh normative for the American Left. Although the American Communist movement never attained a status of even minor importance, and the various professedly socialist groups remained on the fringe of society also, Marxism and crypto-Marxism have been very much with us and are in no serious danger of disappearing. One is tempted to repeat the tragi-comic jest that in a short time Communism and its allies will have totally disappeared from the face of the earth, except at certain American universities and in some circles of New York intellectuals.

On the opposite end of the spectrum is a frequently confused melange of nineteenth century Protestant fundamentalist Christianity mixed with the economic outlook of the Industrial Revolution. As the Left hides behind shibboleths of concern for the disadvantaged and other *human* values, so the Right spouts clichés of tradition and of *family* values, by which it means anything from the work ethic of the last century to sexual repression and the bashing of almost anyone who disagrees with these positions.

Between these two poles move many shades of opinion and allegiance, leaning toward one or the other extreme. This heterogeneous mix of positions is in turn encompassed, ameliorated and to some extent held in check by a system of government older and wiser than any of the shadings of the socio-political spectrum. However, this governmental structure, composed of a threefold division of power parceled out between the executive, the legislative and the judicial branches of government, functions on the basis of a constitution formulated in the eighteenth century, an era in which the ideologies, allegiances and foibles of the present society did not exist in any shape or form.

Who or what, then, is the true America? Who speaks for it? Does the land of the free and home of the brave, the land of opportunity, the nation of the Statue of Liberty have an authentic voice? Or, is the cacophony of voices we hear the only voice of this land and this culture? These are questions worth asking, and to the extent of the available and useful sources of information, this chapter attempts to answer them.

In my view there are three Americas. The first is *Ancient*, or *Shamanic America*, discussed in Chapter 8. The second is *Hermetic America*, which this chapter addresses. The third is *Puritan America*, which in most respects has acted as the opposing force to Hermetic America, which is discussed later in this chapter.

To gain an understanding of Hermetic America, we need to go back a considerable distance in history, to the Alexandrian period of late antiquity. At this time, the Greek god Hermes, son of Zeus, messenger of the gods and patron of communications and commerce, became fused archetypally with the god-form of the Egyptian god Thoth, lord of mind, scribe of the gods and patron of transformation. The result was a splendid mystery system of Gnosis, closely related in spirit to the schools of Christian Gnosticism. A large and deeply inspiring body of mystical literature came into existence, all attributed poetically to Hermes-Thoth and designed to facilitate the spiritual insight, transformation and ultimate liberation of the human soul.

The influence of the Hermetic mysteries asserted and reasserted itself several times in the history of Western culture. After deeply influencing much of early Christian mystical thought in the first four centuries of the Christian era, it returned again in the fifteenth century and, according to historians such as the late Dame Frances Yates, was responsible for the spiritual aspect of the remarkable cultural phenomenon known as the Renaissance. The libraries of Hermetic writings, brought to Italy from Byzantium at this time, were translated under the patronage of the Medici princes and their content publicized to the intelligentsia of Europe by such men as Ficino, Pico della Mirandola and Giordano Bruno. Thus the Middle Ages came to an end amidst the clamor of a newly begun Hermetic Renaissance. (There was another, far less spiritual Renaissance also, known as the "humanistic Renaissance." It was concerned mainly with the revival of classical learning.)

The Hermetic Renaissance was in full swing when Columbus came to America. It flourished in England at the time of Elizabeth I, and thus the immediate ethnic and cultural parent-country of North America became thoroughly "hermeticized" at the very time England was beginning her colonial expansion in the world. Hermetic and neo-Hermetic currents were rapidly transplanted from England to America and were frequently reinforced by the emigration to the New World of European esotericists of a Hermetic orientation, such as German Rosicrucians from Central Europe. From Lord Francis Bacon, the Elizabethan scholar and Hermetic wise man, to Johannes Kelpius, the German mage, and beyond, esoteric influences, largely of Hermetic origin, were brought to bear on the newly founded colonies of North America.

By the time of the American Revolution, the Hermetic Renaissance was fused to a considerable extent with the originally French movement of the Enlightenment. The courts of France, Austria, Russia, and of the German princes were teaming with adepts of the Hermetic arts and teachings. Thus the normative leadership of the American Revolution, particularly its intellectual wing led and exemplified by Benjamin Franklin, was thoroughly imbued with the spirit of the Hermetic Enlightenment.

The founders of the American Republic proceeded to create a model government hitherto unheard of in history, a republic founded on the philosophy of the

Hermetic Enlightenment and expressing, with certain modifications made necessary by the different historical era, the wisdom of the *Corpus Hermeticum* and other Hermetic books. This is how Hermes came to America. Perhaps to the discomfort of some, this chapter argues that the chief inspirer of the American Republic was not Moses or Jesus, and even less Saint Augustine or Saint Thomas Aquinas, but rather Hermes Trismegistus of old. Hermes, who survived among the alchemists, magicians, Rosicrucians, esoteric Freemasons and the French Enlightenment philosophers, crossed the Atlantic on his winged sandals and stood with his caduceus in the first assemblies of the Continental Congress.

There is no doubt that mystical, Hermeticized Freemasonry played a great role in the eighteenth century establishment of a republic on the far side of the Atlantic. The emissary of the revolutionary colonists to France, Benjamin Franklin, was an ardent Freemason, who established close links with leading members of that fraternity at the Lodge of the Nine Sisters in France. There he met the aged Voltaire, whose elaborate Masonic memorial services Franklin attended later. The Lodge of the Nine Sisters counted among its membership Voltaire, Lafayette, Prince Charles de Rohan and the philosopher Helvetius. The Lodge was noted for its occult and Hermetic associations, having been guided at one time by Court de Gebelin, one of the earliest expositors of the esoteric meaning of the Tarot cards. While diplomatic and discreet in voicing his deeper convictions openly, Franklin wrote freely of his Hermetic allegiances and connections in his letters. (See references in bibliography under M. P. Hall.)

Of less direct historical relevance, but of even greater symbolic and archetypal interest are two mysterious occurrences connected with the founding of the Republic. One concerns the design of the flag of the new colonial armies and state. A mysterious individual, never mentioned by name, but often referred to as "the Professor," is said to have appeared suddenly at the committee considering the design of the flag in 1775. He was treated with great respect by Washington and by other highly placed personages of the committee, and exchanged certain signs of recognition with Franklin. He lodged for a while with Franklin and reportedly made predictions concerning the forthcoming recognition of the new American nation by the various governments of the world. This story, based on eyewitness reports, is recounted in *Our Flag,* by Robert Allen Campbell. Even better known is the appearance of a mysterious stranger at the time of the signing of the Declaration of Independence, who gave a rousing speech, motivating many to sign, but who could not be identified or located afterward. The closing words of his address are said to have been: "God has given America to be free!" It is easy to put down such accounts to romanticism and mystery-mongering. Still, archetypal images often appear in inexplicable and synchronistic situations, and their effect is usually impressive and lasting. (See Manly P. Hall, *America's Assignment with Destiny.*)

An unsigned editorial in *The Theosophist* (Madras, India, 1883) attributed to H. P. Blavatsky states: "Yet it is certain though this conviction is merely a personal one, that several Brothers of the Rosy Cross . . . did take a prominent part in the American struggle for independence. We have documents to that effect, and the proofs of it are in our possession." Such words, coming from one of the seminal figures of the esoteric revival of the late nineteenth century, who was herself involved in the work and conversant with the traditions of numerous secret societies of a Hermetic provenance, should not be dismissed lightly.

Hermetic America

The question now arises: What was the content of this Hermetic teaching that was transmitted to the early leadership of the American Republic by various circles of the Hermetic-Rosicrucian-Masonic Enlightenment? To answer this question, we shall begin with a shorthand account, or abbreviated summary, of those points of the Hermetic transmission that have a direct bearing on the founding of the American Republic.

The first of the important principles brought into the fabric of the new commonwealth from the Hermetic Enlightenment was *the separation of church and state.* This principle was unheard of in any part of the world or in any government at the time of the founding of the United States. Under the Constitution, no longer was there an established faith. By law the government completely disengaged itself from the business of religion. The most that religious minorities could expect from other governments up to this time was "tolerance." This meant that, while maintaining an officially established state religion, the authorities would nevertheless patiently endure (*tolerare* means "to endure" in Latin) the exercise of a different religion on the part of some. The prototype of tolerant monarchs was no doubt Frederick the Great, who uttered the famous words: "Let everyone be saved after his own fashion," but still maintained the established Lutheran Church of Prussia. The founders of the American Republic clearly went beyond that.

The popularly advanced theory accounting for the separation of church and state in America is that, since there were several religions present and flourishing in the colonies, it was best to make religion a private matter and thus diffuse potential sectarian dissension. However, in view of the Hermetic influences that were brought to bear on the founders, it might be assumed that this was not the only reason for their attitude. The Hermetic Enlightenment as a whole was not interested merely in the absence of religious strife; rather, it felt that there was something profoundly *wrong* with the theologies of the existing religious denominations in the culture, and that for this reason, none of them ought to be supported. The issue was not so much that one did not know which of the religions was right, but rather that one knew, or at least suspected, that all of them were wrong.

One of the major disagreements between the Hermetic Enlightenment on the one hand and the various denominations of Christianity and Judaism on the other concerned the God concept. All denominations of Christendom at that time, as well as followers of Judaism, were adherents of *theism*, a belief in a personal God, creator, maintainer and judge of the world, who is personally involved in the management of creation at every moment of time. In the eyes of the Hermetic thinkers of the Enlightenment, this concept had shown itself to have not only theoretical flaws, but also to be responsible for certain practical ills, such as the divine right of rulers, the presence of religious law within the fabric of society as well as many more. If God was actively involved in all the affairs of the world and of humans, it was easy to envision that this same God instituted the existing governmental and social structure and that the state ought to enforce God's ordinances in order to please Him. By their separation of church and state, we can infer that the founders of the United States were not in favor of such a God.

The men and women of the Enlightenment were usually not *theists*, but rather *deists*. Deists accepted a Supreme Being as the ultimate origin and the final destiny of all beings and of the universe, but they were convinced that this Godhead did not actively manage the universe or interfere in the affairs of humankind. Theirs was the *Alien God* of the Hermeticists and Gnostics, also known at times as *Deus Absconditus*, "the God who has gone away." (Esotericists of various schools and historical periods shared in this conviction. The aforementioned late nineteenth century figure of the esoteric revival, H. P. Blavatsky, was extremely emphatic in her denial of a theistic concept of God.) The heterodox religious views of many of the founding fathers were not only a matter of privately held conviction: Benjamin Franklin even wrote a liturgy for a new religion based on deistic, Hermetic principles, and sent a copy of it to Jean Jacques Rousseau, who accepted it with pleasure and presumably with approval.

The second distinctively Hermetic feature of the American Republic was the *three branch theory of government*. Although it is not very well known, the United States became and remained in effect a constitutional, elective monarchy, wherein the monarch (named, or misnamed, the "President") has far broader powers than the present constitutional monarchs of Europe. At the time the Constitution was framed, there was even serious debate that the President ought to have the title "Serene Highness," indicating the monarchical character of the office. (Elected monarchs ruling over republics were not unknown in history; the *doge* of the Republic of Venice is an eminent example.) The Hermetic teachings were never predominantly republican, although they were certainly opposed to absolute monarchies. In fact, absolute monarchies were a relatively late phenomenon in Europe; the Holy Roman Emperor, whose office dated back to Charlemagne, was not an absolute monarch, but rather the incumbent of a mystical and mythical office. Monarchs in the Hermetic scheme were regarded as carriers of a remote, ultimate authority, in emulation of the ultimate power of the deistic God. It is likely that persons worshipping the traditional image of God as Jehovah would be unlikely to fashion this kind of Hermetic rulership. However, adherents of Hermeticism know that humans are prone to arrogate to themselves powers and privileges which properly belong only to the true, ultimate God. Such behavior makes people *archons*, which means "intermediate, or secondary, rulers," with overtones of usurpation. The absolute monarchs against whom the Hermetic Enlightenment struggled at the time of the American Revolution were regarded as such *archons*, rather than as authentic representatives of spiritual royalty.

The three branch theory of government separated the executive, legislative and judicial aspects of government, thus preventing the concentration of unlimited power in the hands of any individual or group of individuals. Such a government resembles perhaps nothing more than the structure of the leadership of a Masonic Lodge, with its three principal officers, where the Master of the Lodge holds office by way of election.

Another important Hermetic idea reflected in the founding of America is the *source of the legitimacy of government*. In the prevailing arrangement in Europe at the time, it was understood that the source of legitimacy was the will, or "Grace" of God. However, the founders of American government decided that the will of the people, or "the just consent of the governed," made a government legitimate. Here we find the Hermetic principles powerfully at work again. Ever since Alexandrian Egypt, the Hermetic teachings always gave prominence to the god-like power and dignity of the human soul. The human soul is not a mere creation of God, but rather is divine in origin and in its essential nature, and as such cannot be forever subjected to external authority. The human was constituted as someone who causes events to occur and not as someone who is the passive recipient of the effects of an external divine will. As free agents, citizens may contract with each other to form associations such as state and nation and are not destined to remain subjects of rulers who are foisted on them. (The Social Contract theory of Rousseau also served as one of the inspirations for this feature of American government.)

Finally, one must consider the Hermetic principle of *the alchemical interaction and eventual conjunction of opposing forces*. This principle, more than any other, came to permeate not only American government but the entire history of the United States. The Hermetic vision of existence declares that life is a process, not a fixed condition. Because of this, life cannot be managed, but rather must be permitted to function. In this vision, government is like a master of the alchemical art, who guards and oversees the process, but does not interfere with it. The less governmental interference with the life process of the body politic, the better. If citizens are free to move about, to keep their earnings, to take up trades, professions and engage in business as they choose, the process works. Thus politically, religiously, socially and economically, the existing forces, rather like the alchemical Salt, Sulphur and Mercury, freely interact with each other. The result is growth, transformation and the unfolding of countless, latent potentials of a beneficent nature. The guiding principle of this process is not the petty, obsessive and tyrannical Old Testament God, but rather Hermes, shepherd of the forces of being, the facilitator and wise alchemical transformer of all things.

Puritan America

In contrast to the Hermetic spirit, however, is another element in American life, which from the very beginning was different from and indeed antagonistic toward the Hermetic Enlightenment. This opposing idea was *Puritanism*, or the Calvinistic Protestant form of Christianity. In many ways Puritanism became an entire lifestyle, a powerful force, influencing public life throughout American history.

The Puritan element of American society was originally transplanted here from England. It followed in the footsteps of John Calvin, the theocratic tyrant of Geneva, who was known to put people into prison for such "crimes" as dancing, and was inspired by Calvin's disciple, John Knox, the ranting scourge of Scotland. English Puritans had become the cause of much anguish in their home country. Oliver Cromwell, whose associates cruelly executed King Charles I, instituted a pious dictatorship, in which Christmas was outlawed and merry old England was stripped of virtually all color and beauty. This cruel and boring regime was eventually replaced by the restored monarchy of the House of Stuart, and Cromwell's Puritan friends were increasingly subjected to the ire of just about everybody. Many of them decided to sail over the Atlantic, where they became known as the "Pilgrims" and entered folk legend by way of the first Thanksgiving and other stories.

The Puritans are remembered in sentimentalized literature and art as a harmless sort of immigrant folk who sought religious freedom denied to them in their homeland. However, the truth is that they had denied similar freedom to so many for so long that they were driven out of their homeland as a punishment for very real misdeeds. They soon distinguished themselves in the New World by killing a number of alleged witches, and this at a time when the practice of witch burning had already disappeared elsewhere. Looking to more recent times, it is interesting to note that Dutch Puritans who settled in South Africa became the inventors and perpetuators of apartheid. An altogether unpleasant record, one might say.

Unfortunately, matters did not rest there. Puritan ideology exercised an uncanny influence on practically all of American Protestantism (and one must admit, on much of Irish-dominated American Catholicism also). Not only the direct extensions of the Calvinist tradition, such as the Presbyterian and Reformed churches, but innumerable other ecclesiastical bodies have become saturated with Calvinist ideas and with Puritan values and lifestyle. In innumerable ways, the United States became a very Calvinist country, more so than Switzerland, Scotland and Holland, the original strongholds of this faith. Deism and the Hermetic worldview appealed to the cultural elite, while Puritanism, originally ensconced in New England, spread its principles (modified at times) to the broad masses and to every state.

Whether a Jacksonian Democrat or a Lincolnian Republican, the character of the "common man" of American history always had at least a partially Calvinist element.

Four features of Calvinism (or Puritanism) need to be emphasized here. The first is that the *God-image of Calvinism is Old Testamentary in the extreme.* Luther was the reformer representing Christ, Calvin the one representing Jehovah. It has been wisely noted by C. G. Jung and others that the God people worship places a signature on their psyches. The God-image of the Calvinists is radically at odds with the deism of the Founding Fathers, and its influence has been characterized by harshness, vengefulness and a certain cold-hearted cruelty. (It must be remembered that Calvin and his associates did not avail themselves of the refined and softened theology of later Rabbinical Judaism, in which this God image underwent salutary modifications. Calvin's God came straight out of the Old Testament and out of his *projections* placed upon the same.)

The second point is that *Calvinism is* by nature and history *theocratic* in orientation. Pious dictatorship had been very much a part of the history of this religion. The petty, intolerant and obsessive image of its God was mirrored in the public conduct and policy of its members. Early American history bears abundant testimony to the Calvinist desire to control public as well as private life. Witches were killed, sinners were placed in the pillory or branded with a scarlet letter as part of this syndrome. A fairly direct line runs from Cotton Mather and his clerical judges to such modern movements as the Moral Majority. Clearly, the Hermetic principle of the separation of church and state was never seriously endorsed by the Calvinist mentality.

A portentous feature of Calvinist belief is *the doctrine of predestination.* While originating in abstract theological technicalities, this doctrine came to be universally interpreted to mean that those following the Calvinist ethic were the new "chosen people." Material wealth and success were regarded as the signal hallmarks of divine favor accorded to those predestined for salvation. From this it followed that Calvinists, and those influenced by them, became ambitious, success oriented, and not infrequently ruthless. Euphemistically, this attitude was subsumed under the innocuous term "the work ethic," ostensibly a wholesome, decent and virile creed, which at the same time carried an enormous shadow. This feature of Calvinism soon joined in an unholy alliance with the capitalism born of the Industrial Revolution. The Robber Barons, or unscrupulous businessmen and women of our culture, are not Hermetic but Calvinistic figures. Thus from early times onward, the Calvinist or Puritan spirit countermanded and minimized many of the great advantages the Hermetic spirit had bestowed on America. This tendency has not ceased even today.

Finally, *Puritanism is in fact what we colloquially mean by the term.* It is characterized by extreme moralizing in respect to personal life and conduct, conjoined with considerable laxity when moral principles are applied to politics or business. It implies a joyless, dour attitude toward the pleasurable side of human life on the surface, compensated by fierce greed and a lust for power underneath. (A poignant jest has it that a Calvinist preacher declared that ice cream must have been invented by the devil because it tastes so good.) Depth psychology reveals that this kind of obsessive, repressed lifestyle holds great dangers for the psyche of those who adopt it. At the time of his first visit to the

United States, Jung spoke of this matter in an interview
printed in *The New York Times* September 29, 1912:

> When I see so much refinement and so much sentiment
> as I see in America, I look for an equal amount of
> brutality. The pair of opposites—you find them every-
> where. I find the greatest self-control in the world
> among the Americans—and I search for its cause. . . . I
> find a great deal of prudery. I ask, what is the cause and
> I discover brutality. Prudery is always the cover for
> brutality. It is necessary—it makes life possible until
> you discover the brute and take real control of it. When
> you do that in America, then you will be the most feel-
> ing, the most temperamental, the most fully developed
> people in the world.

The natural result of a lack of self-knowledge is the
exercise of a repressive and judgmental will. Those who
do not know themselves must ever try to control themselves, without knowing whom or what they are attempting to control. The Calvinistic moral attitude is
the direct antithesis of the Gnosis represented by Jung.
Prudery, repression and artificial rules for moral
behavior serve only to hide (at times to fortify) dangerous instinctual forces and psychological complexes in
the unconscious. Thus Jung foresaw many of the future
dilemmas of American culture.

Defending Our Hermetic Heritage

From this vantage point it is clear that the principal
features of Hermetic America and Puritan America
have differences which are portentous and still very
much with us. A profound, and seemingly irreconcil-
able conflict rends the soul of America in two. While in
some subtle ways this conflict may be envisioned as an
alchemical process, it is still incumbent upon those who

perceive the Hermetic heritage of this country to try to defend it and save it from being engulfed by its opposite. Only by recalling and supporting the Hermetic qualities of the American vision will the beneficent alchemical operation envisioned by the founders be permitted to do its work.

What then should be the course of action of those of us who have acquired some information about the Hermetic component of early America and can perceive its value? The answer to this question can be given under three headings.

First, let us recognize the existence of the conflict and consciously understand and articulate its nature and significance. In the legend of the Grail-hero Parsifal, the hero encounters the wounded fisher king Amfortas and asks the ailing archetypal being a simple question: "What ails thee, uncle?" If, like Parsifal, we ask the right question, we too may become the healers of the kingdom. What ails our culture more than any other illness is the continuing, insidious and perilous conflict between the original Hermetic archetypal matrix of the Republic on the one hand, and the Puritan complex on the other. Crime, economic woes, blunders in foreign policy, the human failings of statesmen: all of these are symptoms of the greater, underlying conflict. Will the Hermetic vision prevail? Or will the encroachments of an archaic, unconscious religiosity, and of a gravely flawed worldview and lifestyle based on them, drive the American people and culture farther and farther away from the goals envisioned by those who, inspired by a splendid vision as old as time and as promising as eternity, founded a Hermetic Republic in the land of the uttermost West?

Second, we also need to inform ourselves about the philosophical-mystical roots of Hermetic America and to study our institutions in their light. This task should be easier today than it may have been some years ago. Documents dating back to the early Gnostic and Hermetic flowering of wisdom have become available in recent decades. A significant subculture, often identified as the New Age, is among us, and while it is generally ignorant of its own deeper roots and possibilities, it contains much that is in harmony with the Hermetic spirit of old and may contribute to its revival.

Finally, we need to take our stand and begin vigilantly to sift the Hermetic wheat from the Puritan chaff in contemporary public life. Conservatives ought not to allow themselves to be taken in by slogans and ideas that are not truly conservative at all. Slogans like "Judeo-Christian family values" designed to impose upon the body politic the values and the lifestyle of a Calvinist religious orientation have little in common with the spirit of the Declaration of Independence, the Constitution and the institutions based on these. What we need to conserve in this land is not the baleful heritage of John Calvin, but the spirit bequeathed to us by Washington, Franklin and their fellows. What sane individual could envision Dr. Franklin storming clinics where abortions might be performed? Could Thomas Jefferson sanction the government interfering with the most private activities of citizens in their homes? These men, like other sensible persons everywhere, knew freedom to be one and undivided; they knew that people are either free privately as well as in public, or they are not free at all.

Conversely, liberals ought to cease seeking remedy for all ills in more government, manipulation and interference. The passing of large numbers of laws, as Lao-Tzu recognized, leads to greater lawlessness; the increase of regulations increases confusion and unruliness. Governments do not exist to manage and regulate the lives of citizens but to insure a setting in which the inherent powers and talents of persons can develop and flourish. Every good government in history has been small in size, restrained in the exercise of power and kept at a distance when it concerned the personal, economic and political freedoms and privacy of people. The advancement of commendable causes ought not to be used as an excuse to increase government and to dwarf the freedom and initiative of individuals.

Hermetic America contains the remedy for the ills that have befallen us in this age. The remedy is freedom. With freedom, the alchemy of the spirit corrects the flaws of culture and rectifies the excesses of civilization.

For about a century now, some people in the United States have looked to inferior doctrines imported from unlikely places as the panacea that would solve the difficulties that arise in this land. Fascism, Marxism, anarchism and other schemes too numerous to name have drifted over the seas to be embraced by persons who did not seem to know or care about Hermetic America. Perhaps now, when so many of the unwholesome schemes born of the fevers of the nineteenth and early twentieth centuries have failed, more attention may be paid to the treasure before our eyes. With insight and consciousness, we may rediscover Hermetic America and help it become a reality.

10

Society versus Individuality in America

The title of this chapter might seem incongruous and paradoxical at first glance. For is not the United States the proverbial land in which the individual, individuality and individualism reign? How could such a society, based as it is on the value of the individual, at the same time be at odds with the individual? This question is not easy to answer. Any attempt must be articulated by way of a broad vision spanning centuries.

A Look Backward

As indicated in Chapter 9, the founders of the republic were inspired by a vision of the human being that was infused both outwardly and inwardly with Hermetic and Gnostic principles. Though we hear occasional assertions to the contrary, the worldview of the founders was not the traditional Judeo-Christian one, which ruled European society from about the fifth century onward. In the first three or four centuries, largely under Gnostic influences, Christianity evinced considerable positive interest in the worth of the individual and the concept of freedom that flows from this consideration. However, beginning with the influence of Saint Augustine of Hippo in the late fourth and the early fifth century, this early libertarian Christianity underwent radical changes. Instead of emphasizing human freedom, fortified by the mystery of redemption, Augustine emphasized humanity's enslavement to sin. From these considerations flowed his conviction that humans, irreparably damaged by the fall, could not be trusted to exercise individual autonomy in the moral, religious or political arenas. Elaine Pagels, in her study devoted to the influence of Augustine on Christianity, states the dilemma clearly:

> Are human beings capable of governing themselves? Defiant Christians hounded as criminals by the Roman government emphatically answered *yes*. But in the fourth and fifth centuries, after the emperors themselves became patrons of Christianity, the majority of Christians gradually came to say *no*.
>
> *Adam, Eve and the Serpent*, 98

This *no*, inspired by Augustine, but eventually normative in all of Christendom, led to the creation of a Christian society in medieval Europe that was more collectivistic than individualistic. In medieval European society, the only actual Christian society that ever existed, the worth and the dignity of the individual were not regarded highly. Those who profess that the ideals of the freedom and sovereignty of the individual are somehow based on the Judeo-Christian ethic ignore the clear testimony of history. Western society is not derived from the Judeo-Christian ethic but from the Renaissance and the Enlightenment, eras in which Gnostic and Hermetic values were central.

To prove this point, consider briefly the society of the Middle Ages. This Christian society par excellence was an attempt to realize Augustine's vision of the "City of God." Thus it was hierarchical, static and collective. Its fundamental theory was that God owns the world; people merely administered portions of it. The pope and the emperor were the supreme stewards, administering the known world; they lent kingdoms, princedoms and other dominions to others. No individual truly owned anything; every possession or position was on loan and could be withdrawn. Power, riches and honor came from above; no one possessed such qualities by right. Rulers ruled by "the grace of God" and by the consent of God's stewards. The justification for this position was that humans, even though they may be kings or queens, were in essence only unworthy sinners, upon whom God by grace had conferred power from above. (For more of both the virtues and defects of medieval society, see Chapter 7.)

The collectivist features of this society were numerous. For example, in both the state and the church, the office was always of greater importance than the individual holding the office. While outstanding individuals did appear on the historical horizon from time to time, they were expected to fit into the pre-existing structure of offices and to fulfill the collective purposes of society. The same impersonal features characterized many aspects of the family. Marriages were arranged with virtually no role for personal and romantic love. (The rise of romantic love as part of the troubadour phenomenon had little or nothing to do with orthodox religious principles; rather this phenomenon was generated by distinctly heterodox currents of spirituality with affinity to Gnostic and magical traditions.)

Psycho-historically, these features of medieval Christian society reflect an archaic, largely undifferentiated relationship between the human ego and the unconscious. The unconscious is timeless, and when human life and society are patterned on the unconscious, they tend to become rigid. This statement is not intended to devalue the unconscious. The unconscious is also the source of much creativity, and its dynamics can bring useful change at many levels of human life. By the same token, there is no substitute for a well-developed, psychologically healthy ego. Creativity, flexibility and progress do not depend on either the ego or the unconscious alone, but on creative interaction between the two. In medieval humanity, the ego was largely undeveloped, and as a result, collective patterns influenced by the unconscious ruled.

During the Renaissance, ego development accelerated in Western culture, thus bringing forth the true individual. Why was this so? Unlike Augustine's worldview, the Hermetic vision recognized the individual as a unit of divinity. In the Hermetic view, there is no fall, and thus no personal or collective guilt. In Hermetic terms, one might say that the human being is not a creation of a Demiurge-God, but a spark of the divine fullness. We are not creatures as much as we are creators; not sinners, but gods in exile awakening to the consciousness of our true nature by Gnosis. As the result of the spirit of the Hermetic Renaissance, for the first time in over a thousand years, people began to recognize themselves as creators, as creative individuals. An artist was no longer a nameless craftsman in a guild, or a humble monk in a scriptorium, but an individual, demanding and deserving personal recognition. Suddenly, architects had names, unlike the anonymous cathedral builders of earlier years. The individual had arrived!

When Michelangelo signed his name "I, Michelangelo, sculptor," he was acting as a true Renaissance
man; even a century earlier, such individualism would
have been unlikely. In religion, similar voices were soon
heard. Martin Luther's famous statement "Here I
stand, I can do no other" is the cry of an awakened
individual. The Reformation was above all a movement
on behalf of individual faith based on personal religious
experience, even though these values were quickly lost
in the course of its subsequent historical development.

Of course, the shadow side of the rise of individualism soon asserted itself. Machiavelli, for example,
argued that rulers should be allowed virtually unlimited power and should be exempted from moral rules.
The growth of commerce, fueled by individual incen-
tive, started society on the long road toward the
ascendancy of money-power. Moroever, in the wake of
the Reformation, many petty rulers appropriated fief-
doms that they may have only administered by the
grace of pope or emperor. (The many independent
German princedoms and other small, secular states
regarded as personal possessions by their rulers came
into existence in this manner.) Still, the appearance of
the shadow only testifies to the existence of the light; the
great advantages brought by the new individualism
should not be judged harshly because of its abuses.

Some two hundred years after the Renaissance came
the Age of Enlightenment. In this period, the individualistic principle was extended into wider areas and
touched the lives of more people. Not only was the
individual now dignified as artist or genius, but it was
recognized that the individual also possessed *rights.*
While privileges were previously bestowed by grace, it
was now recognized that individuals had rights which
were innate and inalienable. The mere fact that a

person was a human being bestowed on him or her
"le droits humains," human rights. Thus another important Gnostic-Hermetic step was taken. Needless to say,
this phase also had its shadow. Its name was rationalism, the belief that reason should be the basis for establishing spiritual truth. Just as there were really two
aspects to the Renaissance, one Hermetic and the other
"humanistic" (in the sense of looking to classical learning as the potential redeeming factor of culture), so too
there were two sides to the Enlightenment. Rationalism
seemed at first to represent a useful tool against the
murky obscurantism that prevailed in many religious
circles. Philosophers like Voltaire openly proclaimed
rationalistic principles while secretly cultivating Hermetic ideas in the privacy of their chambers and in the
lodges of the secret orders which they joined. Unfortunately, rationalism, like a rampant sorcerer's appren-
tice, ran away from its Hermetic masters and has
caused much mischief, right up to the present time.

The foundation of the United States took place in the
midst of these philosophic struggles. The Hermetic-
Gnostic vision of the Enlightenment—with its attention
to creativity and to the spiritual dignity and, consequently, the rights of human beings—now had a
chance to build its own sacred land. Not only did the
people have rights, but people were declared sovereign
and were regarded as the source of legitimate authority
in the state. (This issue was discussed in detail in
Chapter 9.)

After the founding of the United States, the forces of
Hermetic individualism on the one hand, and of collectivism on the other, continued to struggle. However,
over time the very fabric of the two opponents changed
in significant ways. Hermetic individualism was increasingly infiltrated by ideas arising from the Indus-

trial Revolution. As a consequence, what was once a genteel, philosophical principle informed by Hermetic insight began to assume a crass, even brutal, materialistic form. Eventually, Hermetic individualism turned into rugged individualism. The enlightened individualist philosopher-statesmen, like Franklin or Jefferson, gave way to the robber barons of industry and business. Some of these new captains of industry gave individualism a bad name. In many instances, business and industry made government subservient to their own ends, but curiously these captains often did not recognize that in doing so, they made a grave mistake. The possibly apocryphal words attributed to a leader of industry are characteristic of this short-sighted attitude: "What is good for General Motors is good for the nation."

Reaction to this hubris soon set in. Collectivism found a new weapon to advance its ends, the ideology of Marx and Engels. This political philosophy pretended to champion the powerless, over whom rugged individualism had ridden roughshod. The great conflict of the twentieth century had begun.

These developments can be summarized as follows:

(1) Sixteenth and seventeenth century: The Hermetic Renaissance creates a spiritual foundation for individualism. This foundation leads to religious, political and commercial individualism, as well as to artistic and cultural developments with individualistic underpinnings.

(2) Eighteenth century: The Enlightenment gives rise to a new Hermetic individualism, based on the recognition of the transcendental potential of the individual. Separation of church and state, the limitation of the powers of government and the inherent rights of the individual are advocated and, in some cases, put into practice, as in the United States.

(3) Nineteenth century: The Industrial Revolution reaches its greatest power. The United States becomes the country epitomizing the industrial age, with all its blessings and shortcomings. Rugged individualism takes the place of Hermetic individualism. Social problems arise to which European collectivist solutions are offered; these solutions are popularized in America by European immigrants. Soon the struggle is between rugged individualism and the new collectivist schemes. The original vision of Hermetic America and its spiritual individualism is almost totally forgotten.

(4) Twentieth century: The struggle between the new collectivism of European origin and private enterprise reaches its highest point between 1917 and the present. Collectivism infiltrates large areas of American life, including education, government and the arts. The level of infiltration reaches impressive proportions when, in the early 1990s, the collectivist system collapses in many of the countries where it was originally established. Confusion arises. Many thinkers begin to look to freedom once more, though a minority doggedly persists in allegiance to collectivist ideas.

The Springtime of Freedom

The last point brings us to the present. It may be no exaggeration that the world today is filled with possibilities which appeared unlikely, if not impossible, even a few short years ago. It is now the springtime of freedom. What will Americans do with it? Though we can hope that the newly emerging world order will lead to smaller countries free from domination by ethnic majorities, along with diminished centralized governments with a lessened appetite for gobbling up the individual rights of citizens, we cannot be certain to what degree these hopes will be realized. Yet to begin to realize some of these high hopes, we Americans must first attain to a clarity of vision, a discerning power which requires a high degree of psychological, and even spiritual development. Such development is not come by easily. It has nothing to do with opportunism or with the mouthing of the clichés to which persons in our culture seem to be addicted. Some such clichés show disdain for "separatism," (no doubt showing the trauma of the American Civil War). Others demand that foreign governments conform in external respects to the American model, as evidenced by the preference shown to republics as against monarchies. (Ironically, all the malign dictatorships of the era just passed were republics.) The remaining portion of this chapter is devoted to some suggestions for how Americans can best make use of this period of new freedom.

Jung insisted that humankind's greatest danger consists in the loss of its individuality in a mass society, under a highly centralized government. These dangers can be avoided, Jung asserted, only through the conscious cultivation of individual awareness, personal moral choices and psychological self-knowledge. Americans have wandered a long distance from the beliefs of the founders of Hermetic America. Collectivism of various kinds, with different ideological underpinnings, is forever assailing us. We are repeatedly taught to look upon ourselves as members of groups or collectivities rather than as individuals. Some of these designations seem innocuous, such as "yuppies" or "baby boomers"; others are more insidious, such as "radical feminists" or "right-to-lifers." But all to some extent limit or circumscribe individual freedom of thought and action.

Marxism, both in its overt expression and in its concealed manifestations, has contributed greatly to the unhappy situation of our psychological collectivization. There is also much impersonal, even inhuman collectivism to be found in many aspects of business and industry, in spite of its operating within the system of free enterprise. Whether we think of ourselves as proletarians (not a very popular form of self-image today), or as members of ethnic or political collectivities, or as employees, company people, or even upwardly mobile members of an affluent society, we are missing the point of our unique individuality.

Jung's *Seven Sermons to the Dead* contains a poignant symbolic statement: "To every blessing of God the Sun the Devil adds his curse." Nowhere is the truth of this statement more evident than in the great psychological upheaval that American culture experienced in the late 1960s and most of the 1970s. Clearly "God the Sun," the light of Gnosis, consciousness and freedom, shone brightly upon many in those turbulent yet creative years. Still, the "devil's curse" was not absent, and its effects are with us still. Marxist collectivist thinking attached itself to many causes and ideologies, often without their advocates being aware of it. For example, the women's movement, youth consciousness, politicized ethnic consciousness and even so-called multiculturalism all contain a good measure of Marxist-inspired collectivism. Following the suggestions of thinkers such as Herbert Marcuse, many people came to accept the artificial division of humanity into antagonistic collectivities, destined to carry on a struggle modeled on the Marxist concept of class warfare. Adapting the class warfare concept to a wide variety of social situations became the chief preoccupation of crypto-Marxist circles throughout the seventies and the eighties. The results are bizarre, with just about everybody envisioning himself or herself as belonging to some kind of oppressed group and adopting an adversary stance toward some other group.

Against these and other blandishments it is especially necessary today to call attention to the pivotal significance of the individual, around which consciousness, society and human history constellate. Before there can be groups, classes or collectivities, there must be individuals. Nothing can occur without the participation of individuals, whether that participation is conscious or unconscious. In *The Undiscovered Self*, Jung described the individual as "a cell in the structure of various international organisms . . . causally implicated in their conflicts." In this respect it does not matter that individuals today often feel consciously that they are powerless victims of uncontrollable forces. In fact, they *are* involved for better or for worse in the activities of the collectivity, even if their involvement is unconscious.

One of the great difficulties, however, is that individuals are often not aware of their unconscious involvements. Depth psychology has been in existence for nearly one hundred years, but in some respects, many people still act as if the unconscious did not exist. Rationalism, born out of the shadow side of the Enlightenment, views the psyche as a sort of shapeless or blank entity born into this world, that can be turned by appropriate environment and education into whatever the dominant societal powers may wish. Because we are so unaware of these influences, we can be victimized by archaic cultural-social ideas and practices, which fail to take into account and provide an outlet for the nonrational, unconscious impulses of the psyche. The result is more individual unconsciousness and less self-knowledge. The unacknowledged unconscious impulses are then repressed and distorted, and instead of being expressed in an acceptable manner in the personal lives of individuals, they sink into the collective unconscious, from which they emerge as dangerous psychic epidemics and mass psychoses.

This process gave rise to the great totalitarian evils of our era, such as German National Socialism and Soviet Communism, but they also play a significant role in the widespread addiction to destructive drugs and other social evils. Moreover, the great hope of an earlier period of American history, the system of free public education, is increasingly proving a failure, thus contradicting the great rationalist contention that we will save our culture by way of education. At the height of its material power, our civilization and culture is imperiled because of its lack of awareness of psychological forces which require individual rather than collective solutions.

The Challenge of Freedom

The clear dangers to both society and the psyche of collectivist thinking make it imperative that individuals in contemporary America examine and become responsive to the personal and collective powers of the unconscious.

The individual's first task is to become aware of the shadow. So much is being written today about the shadow that the concept itself is beginning to seem like a cliché. Still, the shadow is real, and an individual leaves it out of his or her calculations only at great risk. Since the unconscious (like the conscious) is both personal and collective, there is also a collective shadow, which can be defined as the unrecognized, incompatible side of a social collectivity, such as a group or nation. America has unique problems with its collective shadow. These are largely the result of the continuing conflict between the Hermetic and Puritan strains of the national psyche discussed in Chapter 9. The Hermetic worldview can be described as existential; it recognizes the dark and flawed character of many aspects of existence and strives for a liberating Gnosis in the midst of these circumstances. The Puritan view, on the other hand, tends toward guilt. Since the world is envisioned as having been created by a righteous Deity, such flaws as appear in earthly existence must be the fault of human beings. Thus guilt over our individual and collective shortcomings is a common condition. Americans have a constant tendency toward pragmatism and practically motivated actions on the one hand, and toward guilt on the other. The frequent pattern in our society is ruthless, practical action followed by nagging guilt.

Because we cannot face the shadow, we invent compensations designed to minimize our ever-present guilt. Thus the lives of many in this culture are spent in attempts to prove to themselves that they really are good persons, no matter how much evidence exists to the contrary. Fads and fashions of a socio-political character, which tend to inflate issues and elevate individuals to positions of importance which they do not deserve, are usually motivated by dynamics resulting from the unacknowledged shadow. When we Americans promote causes ranging from pop-psychological seminars to the ingestion of wheatgrass as panaceas for the ills of our culture, we are more often than not whistling in the dark of our own shadow. Sigmund Freud stated once that he hoped psychoanalysis would not become popular in America, for Americans would make it into a religion. But while faddish attitudes may temporarily allow us to do what contemporary jargon describes as "feeling good about ourselves," the guilt and anxiety stemming from the shadow always return.

Another step is what might be called the "demystification" of sociology and politics. Based on the assumptions of rationalism, many people have looked to politics as the source of potential redeeming solutions to the perplexities and sorrows of life. The great totalitarian ideologies of recent times were in fact pseudo-religions which wore a political disguise. For example, Hitler's rallies showed a disturbing similarity to evangelical revival meetings. The public brainwashing techniques employed by Maoist China also remind one of malign religious indoctrination. At the present time, much of the faith, enthusiasm and expectation that people used to place at the disposal of political movements is being withdrawn. The bottling up of religious instincts and their diversion into political loyalties is slowly coming to an end. In a profound and important sense, it is not only the ideal of the almighty state and the omnipotent government that has failed, but the notion of politics itself as the central concern and chief preoccupation of men and women.

This withdrawal of psychic energy from socio-political concerns ought to have a salutary effect upon American life. As the spiritual interests that are beginning to replace political preoccupations move toward a more individual and introverted path of expression, the likelihood increases that some of the lost Hermetic vision of America might be recovered. When those tensions and conflicts in the souls of individuals that rightly have an unconscious rather than a political cause are no longer projected into the political process, the legitimate political process will be freed of a difficult and distorting component.

Today, evidence points to the possibility of a change

in America that may be more than superficial. Communications have increased tremendously, thus facilitating a worldwide exchange of ideas among cultures that once seemed impossible. Many have become disillusioned with political ideologies and with purely political solutions to the problems of modern life. Moreover, the convenient projection of the collective shadow of America onto the Soviet Union has been rendered impossible by the radical transformation of this longtime enemy into a somewhat pathetic petitioner for American friendship. A certain scepticism about progress, materialism, science and the essential goodness of the world and human beings promises to restore a more inward-looking and realistic attitude on the part of many. The search for psychological wholeness and for the experience of transcendence, first advanced in the sixties, is still with us. The myth of consciousness is again engaging our attention.

11

America and the New Myth
of Consciousness

One of the more interesting phenomena in the cultural
life of America in recent years has been the rediscovery
of the nature and value of myth. Precipitated in part by
the six-hour series of films for television, based on conversations between Joseph Campbell and Bill Moyers in
1985 and 1986, a great resurgence of interest in mythology has swept the nation and is still not abating. As a
result, myth has once again become a respected avenue
to meaning, employed for that purpose by an increasing
number of artists, film-makers, spiritual teachers, as
well as ordinary men and women in our society.

The mythic revival is all the more remarkable because myths were held in rather low esteem by many
leaders of learning and culture for a long time. Science,
we were told, was interested only in *fact*, which it
ascertained by way of research, while religion was said
to be devoted to *faith*, by which was meant belief in
what we could not know. Between fact and faith there
was not much room left for myth. This condition led to
a great impoverishment of our culture. Looking at the

199

past, we find that every viable society possessed a central, living myth, and that when this myth was damaged, the society in question suffered, sometimes to the point of disintegration. History tells us that in the past, people were provided with a reason for living not by their knowledge of fact, nor by their systems of belief, but by their containment in a myth that played a central role in their culture.

It is also useful to remember that myths were important not only to people from archaic cultures, who had a relatively low level of psychological differentiation and intellectual development. The Greeks, who were excellent myth-makers and also possessed keen intellects, engaged in intellectual distillations of mythic themes, known to them as "theories." (Derived from the verb *theorein*, meaning "to look about in the world," the word meant something like our "world-view.") While the less conscious strata of Greek society may have lived their myths more or less unconsciously, the intelligentsia articulated the myths and amplified them intellectually so that they became theories, or ways of viewing the world.

Unlike the Greeks, Americans no longer have a viable, functioning myth. They are not alone in this calamity, for most major world cultures are moving toward a state of complete or partial absence of myths. Jungian writer Edward Edinger describes the result in *The Creation of Consciousness:*

> The breakdown of a central myth is like the shattering of a vessel containing a precious essence; the fluid is spilled and drains away, soaked up by the surrounding undifferentiated matter. Meaning is lost. In its place, primitive and atavistic contents are reactivated. Differentiated values disappear and are replaced by the

elemental motivations of power and pleasure, or else the individual is exposed to emptiness and despair. (9–10)

Jung and the Myth of Consciousness

Jung himself first formulated the problem of modern humanity existing without myths. In *Memories, Dreams, Reflections,* Jung wrote that in 1912, just prior to his departure from Freud's circle, he came to recognize that he was living without a myth that he could consciously articulate. The Christian myth, as understood by mainstream churches, was no longer meaningful to him, and he had not found any other as yet (192). Years later Jung consciously discovered his own myth (it was of himself as a sort of Gnostic magician, patterned on Merlin), and he lived a long and creative life inspired by this personal myth.

Jung's experience with his own lack of myths, and his subsequent discovery of a personal myth may, perhaps, be taken as an indication of what could be done collectively by our culture if it employed its powers toward such an end. As an individual suffering from the lack of a personal myth may discover one, and thereby discover much meaning and creativity, so too an entire culture, after long years of alienation, may make a discovery of a similar nature and profit by it beyond measure. It is certainly possible that the recent revival of interest in myth in America heralds the beginning of a process during which a new myth might be discovered. It is also possible that the myth we discover may be similar to the one Jung found in the course of his own life, which some regard as a paradigm of the search of contemporary humanity for its myth. As such, Jung's statement on the nature of this myth is especially significant:

Our age has shifted all emphasis on the here and now, and thus brought about a demonization of man and his world. The phenomenon of dictators and all the misery they have wrought springs from the fact that man has been robbed of transcendence by the shortsightedness of the super-intellectuals. Like them he has fallen a victim to unconsciousness. But man's task is the exact opposite: to become conscious of the contents that press upward from the unconscious. Neither should he persist in his unconsciousness, nor remain identical with the unconscious elements of his being. . . . As far as we can discern the sole purpose of human existence is to kindle a light in the darkness of mere being.

Memories, Dreams, Reflections, 326

Amplifying this statement in his *Answer to Job*, Jung wrote: "Existence is only real when it is conscious to somebody. That is why the Creator needs conscious man even though, from sheer unconsciousness, he would like to prevent him from becoming conscious." Consciousness—to become and to remain conscious—and thereby to illuminate the darkness of existence, even the darkness of God: this seems to be the essence of Jung's new myth.

In an extensive discussion in his autobiography, Jung gives certain indications of the higher methodology by which this myth may be implemented, and more importantly, of the goal the process is designed to reach (338). As he does elsewhere, Jung employs alchemical language to describe the objective of the myth. The *coniunctio oppositorum*, or "union of the opposites" as the result of the psycho-spiritual process of alchemy, reconciles not only the human and the divine, but more importantly—and astonishingly—the opposites within the God-image itself, such as the Creator's unreconciled tendencies toward wrath and mercy. Jung considers this ultimate reconciliation, this rectifying of the fault within the image of Deity, as the culmination of the great work of human consciousness: "[T]hat is the meaning of divine service, of the service which man can render to God, that light may emerge from the darkness, that the creator may become conscious of His creation, and man conscious of himself."

Those not intimately acquainted with Jung's thought, or, more importantly, with the archetypal background of his ideas drawn from ancient Gnosticism, may find these statements difficult to comprehend. In essence, Jung is saying that the purpose of human existence is consciousness, or as it was once called, Gnosis. To the Gnostics and to Jung, the Creator was not the same as the ultimate, transcendental Godhead. (A similar distinction is drawn in the Kabbalah and in the theosophical teachings of H. P. Blavatsky.) While the ultimate Godhead *is* pure consciousness, the lower, Creator God (Demiurge) is alienated from its origins, and thus lacking in consciousness. It follows that although human beings are inferior to the Creator in size and power, they are superior to the Creator in their consciousness. By becoming ever more conscious—by achieving Gnosis—human beings can increase the consciousness of the Creator. To Jung, "consciousness" meant being aware in the psychological sense. Such consciousness involves a responsiveness to both the conscious and unconscious aspects of being and the self. Once these unusual ideas about God became known, Jung attracted a considerable number of enemies, especially from the ranks of the clergy. Still, he insisted on giving voice to his Gnostic psycho-theology. My purpose in this chapter is to make Jung's myth more comprehensible, and more important, to present a step-by-step outline of the process by which his myth can be practically implemented.

The all important, salvific task of humanity, according to Jung and the Gnostics, is to increase our consciousness. We not only *ought* to become conscious (after all other tasks and projects have been attended to, as it were) but we *must* become conscious, not only for our own sakes but for the redemption of the world, the universe, indeed of God. The word "conscious" is derived from the Latin *con* or *cum*, meaning "together," and *scire* meaning "to know," "to apprehend." The combined meaning is therefore "to know together." The cognate term in German (the original language of depth psychology) for the noun "consciousness" is *Bewusstsein*, derived from *wissen*, "to know." These expressions each have a definite relation to the Greek *Gnosis*, the oldest and most distinguished synonym for "consciousness," in its psychological meaning.

To demonstrate the depth of the term, consider a few early definitions of consciousness, given by ancient Gnostic teachers at a time when "consciousness" was known as "Gnosis." In the second century, Theodotus defined "Gnosis" as the knowing of "who we were, and what we have become; where we were . . . whither we are going; from what we are being released; what birth is and what is rebirth." The Gnostic Monoimus wrote: "Abandon the search for God and for creation and other external matters. Look for [Gnosis] by taking thyself as the starting point. Learn who is within thyself, who it is who makes everything his own and who says: 'My God, my mind, my thought, my body.' Learn the sources of sorrow, joy, love, hate . . . if thou carefully investigatest these matters thou wilt find that this one is within thyself." A contemporary scholar of Gnosticism Gilles Quispel often translated "Gnosis" as "self-knowledge." These definitions come very close to what Jung and other depth-psychologists call "consciousness." Also, just as modern psychologists came to use the term "consciousness" as denoting the opposite of "unconsciousness," so the Gnostics stated that Gnosis is the opposite of *agnosis*, that is, "non-knowing" or "unconsciousness."

Preliminary Considerations

Before the myth of consciousness can become an operative process within the individual two preliminary changes must occur. First, there must be a certain disillusionment of the mind. In other words, the illusion that the present existential condition is sufficient and satisfactory must be dissipated. The recognition may be experienced as a sense that something is wrong. This recognition may be expressed as follows: There is a flaw in life, in my life, in everyone's life. There is a flaw in the world, in my world, in everyone's world. Religious faith, philosophical reasoning, technological skill, artistic and aesthetic beautification, can no more remedy this flaw than can power or wealth, sensory stimulation or instinctual gratification. When all is said and done, when all things have been tried, the fault is still present.

In theory, we could arrive at this recognition easily in America. In practice, however, obstacles such as the belief system of Puritan America mitigate against it. The Puritan ethos says, "The earth is the Lord's and He made it." Thus it would be sacrilegious to assume that the world created by God could be flawed. A second factor mitigating against the recognition is the almost adolescent enthusiasm of the American psyche, which assumes that things are either all right the way they are, or if they are not, then they can assuredly be fixed. Most Americans, whether religious or humanist, conservative or liberal, share in this assumption, this optimism of doing. If we do good, the Good God will help us, implies religion. If we work hard, save our money, show a maximum degree of individual enterprise and fortitude, the world will improve, say most conservatives. If we manage things well at the governmental level, if we pass enough laws, spend enough tax money, the world will be just fine, say the liberals. But when all is said and done, as noted earlier, the flaw, the fault is there; it has not been rectified at all.

Americans need to learn that not all things can be fixed, that not all things can get better if we just *do* something about them. In some cases we must recognize that the nature of the difficulty is such that doing something won't help. In even more cases we must come to understand that *the doer must change before his doing can be effective.* A Chinese sage said, "If the wrong man employs the right means, the right means work in the wrong way." In terms of the Jungian myth, we may say that the doer must be conscious, otherwise he or she will not so much do as undo. The twentieth century has furnished abundant proof of the truth of this principle at the collective level. Flawed, unconscious thinking at the peace conferences after both world wars resulted in peace which inevitably spawned war as well as oppression (see the Epilogue). We have *to be* before we can *do*, and in our case that means we must be conscious.

The second preliminary recognition we must come to before adopting the myth of consciousness as our operative process is that the essential wrongfulness of our existential condition is not anyone's fault, not even our own. Faultfinding is a form of negative projection which at best can give us only an inadequate picture of the dynamics of events and conditions. Our parents, our society, our political and economic system are not truly at fault when it comes to our existential predicament. Neither can Judeo-Christian sin and guilt explain our condition. It is time we declare that we are not sinners, that we are not guilty. We may commit unfortunate deeds and be responsible for personal misdemeanors, but the great, fundamental matters that are wrong with existence are not the fault of human beings. Once we have come to recognize that something is radically wrong, and that we cannot blame anyone for this wrongness, we will be ready to take the first step on the road to consciousness. The new myth will be operative rather than merely theoretical.

Actualizing the Myth of Consciousness

The first step in the actualization of the myth of consciousness is that we permit the destruction of the universe in which we have existed. More often than not this involves primarily a "relativation" of our "personal" reality. The word "personal" means that just as our perception of reality is our own, so too its altering must be confined to our own selves. "Relativation" implies that this process is not an extinction of old values, but rather a process which renders relative the concepts and values which we previously considered to be absolute. Specific values increase, while general values decrease. Concrete realities become more important than abstract principles. While this may seem a terrible thing to say, as a result of this process, we become, in a certain sense, unprincipled. What actually happens is that when reality takes over, abstractions are reduced to their proper size. When we enter the practical realm of the myth of consciousness, we enter the fluid, mercurial realm of psychic reality, where all rules engraved in stone are inappropriate. Attachment to rigidly held abstractions, to theories and doctrines of any variety, diminishes and eventually vanishes. What remains is the living reality of the deeper psyche, operating from its own vision and guidance.

This kind of spiritual pragmatism seems quite compatible with the American psyche. Pragmatism has always been one of the more prominent and admirable features of the thinking of Americans. Never mind what sounds good in theory, Americans often say; what matters is what works in practice. This attitude is related in many ways to the Hermetic spirit of the early republic, which was envisioned as a great experiment of history, a practical testing ground of freedom. Opposing Hermetic flexibility and practicality, however, is the rigid, Old Testament inclination toward abstract principle and law that characterizes Puritan America. Thus Americans are at once the most pragmatic people, and also the people who enact more written laws than any nation on earth. "There ought to be a law!" is a statement voiced whenever a perplexing or unsavory situation arises. Hopefully, the Hermetic component in the American psyche will eventually win out over the Puritan element, and facilitate the kind of permeability and intuitive pragmatism that is required for the myth of consciousness to take hold.

The second step in the enactment of the myth is the entry of the psyche into the process of creative conflict. This means that we must leave behind our attachment to the current overvaluation of tranquility or lack of conflict, and also to the overvaluation of health, wealth and power. One of the ways that this change may be approached is by contrasting the conditions of a static state with those of a process. We must recognize that tranquility, peace, health, wealth and power are all descriptions of states or conditions. They are not processes. Consciousness, on the other hand, is a process, not a state of being. This brings up the issue of commitment. To what is an individual committed in an active pursuit of the myth of consciousness? The commitment must always be to the process and never to the outcome. Persons, symbols, ideas and ideals can all find their proper places within the process, but the process itself must be regarded as primary, other goals as secondary.

As old certainties are dissolved in the first phase of the process, the burden of creative conflict is necessitated by the second. This task presents difficulties to any psyche, but particularly to the American psyche. The dialectic process has never been high on the agenda of education or of social interaction in America. A certain personalized ego-relatedness common to Americans has always tended to assume that if someone disagrees with our point of view, it is an assault upon our personhood. That truth could be discovered by the process of debate was never a particularly popular belief to most people, with the possible exception of courtroom lawyers. Political debates between candidates for office as well as debates in Congress often take place, but their object is hardly ever the discovery of truth but rather political advantage. Most of us are reluctant to place our ideas and convictions on the chopping block of the dialectical process. Similarly, it seems that our psyches are exceedingly vulnerable to interior conflict and that the conflict inherent in the dialectical process precipitates depression and other neurotic symptoms very easily. These conditions of the American psyche do not augur well for transformation within the myth of consciousness.

The role of creative conflict in increasing consciousness may be apprehended more easily if we contemplate the phases of the classical Greek drama. The first phase is battle or conflict, in which the antagonists encounter each other. The second phase is defeat, in which one or more of the protagonists is vanquished, and usually killed. The third phase is the lamentation, in which the chorus, with great emotion, mourns for the defeated and dead heroes. The fourth is the coming of a god, the proverbial *deus ex machina*, who is mechanically lowered to the stage, and who brings about the dramatic resolution of the conflict. The lessons to be learned from this scheme for our purposes are twofold. The first is that the essence of the drama of the soul is growth through conflict. The creation and enlargement of consciousness cannot take place without the creative alchemy of conflict. The second lesson is that in the conflict we may need to experience defeat and lamentation before the archetypally facilitated resolution can occur. If the process is interrupted when it becomes dark and painful, the chances are lessened that the resolution we desire will come about.

Thus by the conflict of will and counterwill, of yes and no, affirmation and negation, and in the ultimate resolution of these conflicts brought about by the wisdom of the archetypal psyche, consciousness is born and expands. Moral opposites are very much part of this process, so that the psyche is forced to make choices that are not dictated by external commandment but by individual, conscious insight. The objective of this process is not moral goodness, but conscious wholeness of the psyche.

At this point, we come to another predicament. Since in the course of the pursuit of the myth of consciousness we cannot follow the accustomed moral impulse to espouse one opposite as against another (not even good against evil), we no longer have the luxury of feeling righteous. We are, in fact, no longer "good" men and women. Nor can we "feel good about ourselves" which, as noted in Chapter 10, has become one of our favorite preoccupations in recent years. Instead, we must become alchemical vessels in which light and darkness, good and evil, male and female struggle, embrace, commingle, fuse, die, and are born. All our cherished ethical beliefs—monotheism, the belief of Jews and Calvinists that they are chosen people, predestined for righteousness—vanish before our eyes. Our moral superiority also evaporates. Not only are we no longer able to condemn others we may consider unrighteous, but we are also not able to condemn that side of ourselves that we have been taught to despise and abominate. We are obliged to love our neighbor, and we must also love our selves, in full recognition of the potential for evil within. In this self-accepting love, we discover the great secret concealed in the admonition to "love thy neighbor as thyself."

The third step in the actualization of the myth is the conjunction of the opposites which follows their conflictual interaction. This step represents the best mechanism for the generation of consciousness. When the union of opposites occurs, consciousness is born. Unfortunately, this event is easier to experience than to explain. However, we do, in fact, experience this reconciliation frequently in our lives. Leisure and work, altruism and self-love, youthful energy and mature wisdom, idealistic self-sacrifice and common sense frequently wrestle and conjoin within us, thus bringing us to more highly developed states of consciousness.

One of the chief polarities in human life is the polarity between masculine and feminine. The reconciliation of anima and animus is one of the chief tasks of the individuation process (see Chapter 3). The conjunction of the opposites of the male and female parts of ourselves reminds one in certain ways of the Gnostic mystery of the bridechamber, in which the human self is sacramentally joined to the divine Self. These mystery rites were always envisioned as a form of marriage, a *hieros gamos*, "holy matrimony." An insightful modern description of this phenomenon can be found in *Androgyny*, by June Singer:

> Androgyny is not trying to manage the relationships between the opposites; it is simply flowing between them. One does not need to ride the rapids, one can *become* the rapids. One does not need to do anything but flow between the Masculine and Feminine, touching both, yielding to all obstacles and thereby overcoming them. . . . The person who has become the androgyne, the hidden river that has risen to the surface, finds his or her own level and makes an impression on the world without any special effort to do so. Water is gentle, yet it wears away rock. It is strong because it is not opposed by nature; nor does nature go against it. And so it can be with the person who chooses the way of the androgyne.

Those persons who have undergone the interior marriage become psychically androgynous. The true sign of wholeness is that the two primary polarities, the masculine and feminine, have combined in an interior harmony. It would be premature to speculate on the possibilities for developing such intrapsychic androgyny in American culture. Yet in some ways the process may have started already. The radical changes in the roles and attitudes of the sexes and the breaking down of rigid stereotypes of gender point toward such possibilities. Though these external changes are important, we must realize that the myth of consciousness in its various phases has to be lived internally. The dangerous extroversion of our culture always places temptations in our way, which often detract from the interior work of our souls. If these temptations are successfully overcome, the future actualization of this step of the myth seems promising.

The fourth and last step of the myth is the one alluded to earlier in connection with the ideas voiced by Jung in *Answer to Job*. Edward Edinger called this step "the transformation of God." Admittedly, this concept is subject to much misunderstanding. As noted earlier, the God referred to here is the Creator-Demiurge of the Gnostics, not the Deity worshipped by the mainstream religions of the West. Our confusion comes when we hear Jung use words which have traditional connotations in our culture. Jung, we must remember, insisted also on an intimate relationship to join the God-image with the archetype of the Self. (Though it may seem strange, this concept is not unlike the one taught by Saint Paul when he spoke of "Christ in us, the hope of glory.") Moreover, unlike the Gnostics who remained silent about the possibility that the Demiurge could be redeemed, Jung time and again affirmed that the Creator-God could be redeemed by becoming conscious, and that this process could be facilitated by humanity. While mainstream Christianity holds that God redeems human beings, Jung held that humans could redeem God. The question is how can this redemption be accomplished?

God's (the Demiurge's) unconsciousness, Jung said, has one primary manifestation—the loss of its feminine side. In *Answer to Job*, Jung wrote that the Creator-God once had a feminine side who was his sister, consort and possibly his mother all at once, and that her name is Sophia, which means "wisdom." By losing contact with Sophia, God became unwise or, in psychological terms, unconscious. Thus it is evident that the Creator-God's way to consciousness leads to the feminine, which he needs to recognize and to rehabilitate, and with which he must achieve union.

Jung's spiritual feminism is not sufficiently appreciated by most people in our culture. His approach was subtle, psychologically mature and in no way politicized, qualities which distinguish him rather sharply from many writers who address themselves to the subject of the feminine in the present era. Still, Jung's approach is worth inquiring into, for it is based on his vast empirical experience with the psyche and his equally vast insight into the psychological relevance of such protopsychological and protofeminist symbol systems as Gnosticism, Hermeticism, alchemy and others.

In our time, when people have begun to ask if God could be a woman, few remember that it was Jung who said, about seventy-five years ago, that in the distant past, God probably had been a woman. Building on the theories of nineteenth century scholar J. J. Bachofen, Jung advocated the idea that before 4500 or 4000 B.C., a matriarchal culture worshipping a mother goddess probably functioned in Europe and some of the Mediterranean region. Subsequently, Jung's disciple Erich Neumann wrote several studies of psychohistory, in which he developed the theory of the four phases of individual (and possibly also collective or cultural) psychological development: the ouroboric, matriarchal, patriarchal and integral phases. Joseph Campbell and other mythologists following in Jung's and Neumann's footsteps popularized the notion of the "Age of the Great Mother," thus building a foundation for the theories of the many feminist and feminist-influenced writers of our day.

We need to recall, however, that Jung was never particularly invested in the historical accuracy of Bachofen's theory; he merely felt that it made *psychological sense* in terms of the patterns of the growth and development of the individual human psyche. We also need to remember that when Jung's early mentor, Freud, tried his hand at amateur anthropology in such works as

Totem and Taboo and *Moses and Monotheism*, he succeeded only in making himself ridiculous. History and psychohistory are not the same thing.

Jungians might heed Freud's sad example and exercise restraint in endorsing the historical accuracy of the currently popular notions about the Goddess and the postulated matriarchy in which she is presumed to have reigned. Scepticism has been mounting regarding these theories in scholarly circles, in spite of their wide acceptance in many places outside of conventional scholarship. According to an increasing number of highly respected scholars—among whom are Swiss scholar Walter Burkert and the University of Chicago's Wendy Doniger—although feminine figurines have been found in large numbers in Neolithic sites, there is no clear-cut evidence that these came from sanctuaries that were dedicated to a unitary goddess, or that the goddesses worshipped were not considered to be part of a polytheistic system. Neither is there any conclusive evidence that the worship of goddesses was in any way conjoined with political systems of a matrifocal nature. Commenting on these lacunae in evidence, Burkert wrote, "Consequently the Mother Goddess interpretation has come to be regarded with increasing scepticism."

The significant conclusion that needs to be drawn for our purposes is that, while the wholeness that needs to be brought to the Creator requires rescuing and elevating the Divine Feminine, this task need not be wedded to historical and anthropological theories which are highly speculative. Thus, bringing wholeness to the lonely, irascible and in part unconscious male Creator-God is not a political task, but a psychological one, and even a spiritual one. The problem with this task, as Jung very bluntly stated, is that "America is extroverted as hell." The ability of people in our culture to address themselves consistently to tasks that are psychological and therefore internal is regrettably small. Money, prestige and power are goals that appeal strongly to the extroverted psyche; psychological transformation does not. This extroverted mentality has time and again yielded to the blandishments of such influences as Marxism (and also to the material gains offered by the profit system), and has succeeded in transposing the concept of class warfare into areas where its applicability is even less legitimate than it was in its original context.

Thus we must recognize that the issue of God versus Goddess is not about class warfare or political power, but rather about psychological and ultimately metaphysical wholeness. Those people who recognize this clearly and are willing to act upon it will be the true heroes of consciousness. They will help to restore wholeness and create consciousness in the souls of men and women, and beyond that, in the subtle, metaphysical dimension of gods and goddesses. To quote Edinger again: "As it gradually dawns on people, one by one, that the transformation of God is not an interesting idea but is a living reality, it may begin to function as a new myth. Whoever recognizes this myth as his own personal reality will put his life in the service of this process." (*The Creation of Consciousness*, 113)

With this we complete the last stage of the process which implements the myth of consciousness. The four stages of the process are, in essence, a profound, internal alchemy which is very much needed in our world, in our humanity, and if we are to believe Jung, in the nature of God. Will this need be met in our day? Will the people of America, with their long tradition of freedom and of the value of the individual, play an important role in meeting this need? These are questions which may be more easily asked than answered. The answer will be given by history, and within the historical frame, by men and women of flesh and blood transforming their individual psyches. The essence of these considerations, however, is freedom. In the past, we tried to be free without consciousness, and freedom changed into its opposite before our eyes. Moreover, when we struggled for consciousness under conditions lacking in freedom, we fared ill. Perhaps now the time is ripe to combine freedom and consciousness. Such is my hope.

Epilogue:
Thoughts on a Possible
New World Order

At the dawn of the twentieth century, optimism ran high that the 1900s would be the most beneficent century the world had ever witnessed. Science, financial growth, rapid industrialization and prospects for international peace engendered such high hopes that the future looked promising indeed. As history unfolded, however, a very different picture was revealed. Two devastating world wars, the Great Depression, and the rise of totalitarian dictatorships of unprecedented power and malice—including Nazi Germany and the Marxist giants Soviet Russia and Communist China—brought untold suffering. Now, as the twentieth century draws to a close, the possibility has arisen once again that we may be able to make good on the optimism which prevailed at the turn of the century. At this critical juncture, it may be useful to ask two questions: What went wrong early in the century? And, conversely, what is beginning to go right now, at the conclusion of the 1900s?

In answer to the first question, we might say that the

219

world order that emerged after the two world wars largely left one crucial element out of its calculations: freedom. In spite of the glib slogans about the self-determination of nationalities voiced at the peace conferences after World War I, many small nations were forced into empires and miniempires, in which their lot was unhappy. The current disintegration of the Russian empire and the strife erupting today in Central and East European countries are the result of the artificial creation of multination states at the conferences of Versailles.

Simultaneous with the building of multinational states was an unprecedented emphasis on the importance of centralized government. While nationalities were disenfranchised, private individuals lost their freedom to own, produce and trade material goods without government interference. National, economic, political and religious freedoms were all curtailed and, in many instances, completely lost. By the middle of the century, freedom was the most endangered commodity in the world. There were many promises to be sure. German National Socialism promised the expansion of borders (*Lebensraum*), as well as military and industrial might; international Marxism promised the equal distribution of wealth and the establishment of a workers' paradise. None of these promises were fulfilled; what happened instead was the loss of freedom in many areas of life.

The late 1980s and early 1990s brought a dramatic reversal of the trends that dominated the earlier decades of the century. This reversal was largely brought about by the failure of centralized government. Today, communist and other totalitarian governments are losing control. As their people are granted some freedoms, they desire more. Walls that held millions of men and women captive are crumbling; borders are being revised; property and profit have become acceptable and even desirable motivations for human endeavors. The desire for individual freedom combined with the moral and economic bankruptcy of the system are conquering the totalitarian conquerors of earlier years.

Not only is the totalitarian variety of Marxism exiting from the stage of history, but also the more moderate forms of centralized economic planning and social engineering are tottering. Until recently, much was heard about the Swedish model of socialism. However, it is likely that from now on, we shall hear less about it than before. In September, 1991, the Social Democratic Party of Sweden suffered a devastating electoral defeat, signaling that after fifty-three years of rule, this advocate of massive income redistribution may be retired for good. Even if the Swedish party rises again at another election, it seems fairly certain that the Swedish model, long praised by sympathizers the world over, will never be the same. It is more than likely that other socialist experiments existing elsewhere will be unable to survive the rigors of the waning of the twentieth century. What went wrong earlier in the century was the lack of freedom. What is going right now is the increase of freedom. It is as simple as that and as amazing.

Alchemical Transformation

These considerations bring to mind a subject that might, at first, seem quite unrelated to such issues as socialism, capitalism, political freedom and the present changes in the world order. This subject is alchemy.

Alchemy was not only a prescientific chemical discipline, popularly associated with making gold. Evidence indicates that the ancient Gnostic notion of spiritual growth through the interaction of creative opposites in the soul was known to some alchemists, notably the third century Gnostic teacher Zosimos. He and other practitioners may have integrated this idea into the art of alchemy. Building in part on this evidence, Jung developed a body of theory that indicates that modern depth psychology also resembles closely the ancient discipline of alchemy, particularly in its use of analysis to bring about psychological wholeness by way of integration.

Underlying alchemical thought is the idea that a spontaneous process of slow growth underlies both life and the structures of the universe. Unrefined and ignoble manifestations of being grow slowly and ripen into nobler and purer forms, by way of an exceedingly slow process of natural growth. A less optimistic version of this theory holds that nature does not so much grow as change, and that no creative change of an ultimately beneficent kind may be expected from this undirected process. Working from these beliefs, alchemists felt that they possessed secrets which would enable them to speed up immeasurably the gradual processes of change existing in nature. The way of nature, they said, is *growth*, while the alchemical way is *transformation*, and there is a great difference between the two.

The principle of natural growth may be illustrated by the example of the development of an oak tree from an acorn. The potential oak is fully present within the acorn, and through a process of linear growth, this potential realizes itself over a period of time, as the seed grows into a seedling, which matures into a tree. Alchemy, on the other hand, works more like the transformation of a caterpillar into a butterfly. At a certain point in the transformational process, the caterpillar spins a cocoon, in which it literally dissolves into a dark mass of inchoate organic substance, possessing neither the qualities of a caterpillar nor those of a butterfly. Then a mysterious reorganization of the dark mass takes place. The result is that a butterfly eventually emerges.

The cocoon, said the alchemists, is the alchemical retort, the vessel of transformation. The body of the caterpillar is the known, natural world, composed of the four elements of earth, water, fire and air. The natural world first undergoes a radical dissolution; it becomes the dark creative mass, the "massa confusa," which is likened to the primeval chaos that preceded the creation of cosmos. This dark mass, which is also known as prime matter, is not a substance with natural growth potential, but a mass with a potential for creative transformation. At this point, the caterpillar-butterfly analogy ends, for the alchemical paradigm now envisions two polar opposites (often called "king and queen," "sun and moon," "sulfur and salt") emerging from the mass of prime matter. The creative and intricate interaction of these opposites eventually brings forth the end result of the alchemical process: the Stone of the Philosophers. The facilitator of this process is a third power, the alchemical mercury, the medium of the conjunction, without which the final phase of transformation could not take place.

Thus we find that in alchemy, creative change is brought about not by linear growth applied to a single principle but rather by the conjunction of two binary opposites which, by combining, produce the result of the "great work." Jung envisioned that the alchemical model of transformation fitted the process of the integrative development of the human psyche exceedingly well. The development of the human psyche from immature fragmentation to individuated wholeness does not follow the model of unidirectional growth, but rather resembles the alchemical work of transformation. In *Psychology and Alchemy*, *Alchemical Studies* and *Mysterium Coniunctionis*, Jung demonstrated in great detail the similarities between the psychological development of the human psyche toward wholeness and the transformational process of the great work of alchemy. The evidence he marshalled in support of his view is convincing. Interestingly, he did not only suggest analogies and correspondences to join depth psychology and alchemy. He also saw that alchemical principles have a relationship to physics and other areas of human inquiry. For example, Jung described the alchemical notion of the subtle bodies of the human being (a doctrine popularized in modern times particularly by the theosophy of H. P. Blavatsky) in his *Psychology and Alchemy:*

> The moment when physics touches the "untrodden, untreadable regions," and when psychology has at the same time to admit that there are other forms of psychic life besides the acquisitions of personal consciousness—in other words, when psychology too touches on the impenetrable darkness—then the intermediate realm of subtle bodies comes to life again, and the physical and the psychic are once more blended in an indissoluble unity. We have come very close to this turning-point today.

Jung's theorizing about the process of transformation and the other features of alchemy suggest that alchemy can be fruitfully applied to many different fields of endeavor, including the natural order and the human mind. In these concluding pages, I should like to suggest another area in which alchemical principles can be applied: human society and its transformation.

The Transformation of Human Society

If we apply the alchemical model to human society, we might envision first of all a process of slow, organic development in which societies follow the linear model of the oak tree. Traditional societies do grow, but so slowly that their growth can be recognized only from the perspective of many centuries, or even millennia. But the mercurial spirit that catalyzes transformational growth is never absent. Time and again, a Prometheus-like figure steals a kind of divine fire that facilitates the transformation of human life and society. Our culture has seen many such leaps of transformation: the conquests of Alexander the Great, the coming of Christianity, the Renaissance, the Industrial Revolution, and in our day, accelerated technological development, with its immense potential to affect and inform the human mind.

Let us consider two of these seemingly alchemical developments in detail. The Industrial Revolution reduced many aspects of life in society to a condition like unformed prime matter. Concepts such as day and night; winter, summer, spring and fall; and many other guideposts which previously circumscribed human life have been made relative, if not rendered insignificant, by a technology with the capacity to defy nature. Modern industrial development has been in many ways a manifestation of what the alchemists called the *opus contra naturam*, the "work of transformation" that, at least in certain respects, "goes against nature" and its innate ways and tendencies.

This dark phase of alchemical transformation is

always envisioned as disorienting, painful and terrifying in its alienating character. But out of the dark "massa confusa," compounded from the smokestacks and slums, and from the disorientation of previously settled class and power structures, arose a number of powerful and ultimately creative alchemical binaries: labor and capital; democracy and aristocracy; conservatism and liberalism; religiosity and atheism, and many more. The dualities struggled and embraced, combined and disengaged, died and were resurrected in prolonged and bewildering sequences of alchemical transformation. At the present time, it seems we are witnessing the entry of humanity into a new transformational phase within this process, the nature of which is explored below.

One aspect of this process of alchemical transformation is of prime importance. That is the fact that the work of social transformation must not be managed or organized externally. An alchemist prepares certain preconditions for the transformation, such as the alembic or vessel of transformation and the slow, steady fire under the vessel, but in all other matters, the process needs to be *allowed* to happen, rather than *made* to happen. Applying this principle to human society, we need to recognize that, if left to its own devices, society will, through conflict and occasional setbacks, recessions, depressions and dislocations, move toward ever greater and more creative achievements. (It goes without saying, however, that insightful and compassionate agencies—hopefully ones of a nongovernmental character—ought to be present to mitigate the human suffering that may be caused by less felicitous episodes within the process of transformation.) Even as the individual psyche must be trusted to work out its own redemption within the process of individuation, so too the creative spirit of collective human endeavor will transform itself through the conflict and eventual reconciliation of social opposites, if society is left to its own devices.

Let us look at some areas in which these principles apply. In the economic marketplace, competition produces more desirable results than does a managed, centrally-planned economy, which lacks competition and profit. (The failure of communist and socialist economies the world over has come about precisely through the neglect of this principle.) In the marketplace of ideas, the best and most creative results always arise when freedom of thought, research and information are fully present. Truths are proven best in the arena of free alchemical interaction. The world has seen too many "thought police" and too much propaganda of one kind or another. Similarly, in the realm of personal behavior, individuals need to work out their own moral alchemy, provided, of course, that people are not harmed by the moral autonomy of anyone else. In this regard, Jung has noted, "There is no morality without freedom."

Here too the analogy between the psyche and society is apparent. When the mind is manipulated, tricked or exploited, it ceases to transform and move toward wholeness. Distrustful of the spontaneous ordering and healing patterns of the psyche, some people are forever trying to order their minds about. The pattern is very much the same whether it exists in psychology, economics, politics or other areas. Those who distrust life must of necessity manipulate it, and the results of this manipulation are uniformly disastrous. As noted earlier, transformation must be allowed to happen; it cannot be made to happen. In this recognition lies the true, psychological justification for freedom, and the reason that all tyranny, no matter how well intentioned, is doomed to failure.

George Orwell, in his prophetic book *1984*, gave the tyrannical, false alchemist of the twentieth century a fitting name: "Big Brother." Implicit in this name is the arrogance and sham-paternalism so freely exercised by dictators like Hitler, Stalin and Mao. Big Brother has been watching the world in this century for more years than anyone cares to remember. Perhaps the time has come at last for Big Brother to retire from the stage. Few, if any, tears will be shed upon his departure.

With the coming of the last decade of the twentieth century, the alchemical transformation of our civilization has entered a new phase. Some have called it a "new world order," a term we might be inclined to accept, provided that we understand that its meaning is different from what the term popularly implies. The new world order will not be a supranational government; it will not be a new ideology taking the place of the disastrous ideologies of the past; it will not establish huge, collective systems to manipulate human beings or to remake the world. Instead, this new phase *must* and hopefully *will be* one that leaves individuals freer than ever before. The coming of this new phase is being heralded by many events that are already in progress.

Promising Signs of the Times

The first of the promising signs of the times, mentioned previously, is the failure of centralized government, as evidenced by the collapse of totalitarian regimes with their characteristic lack of individual and economic freedom. To this must be added the failure of empires, or multinational states, like the Soviet bloc.

The current rise of ethnic nationalism may teach us that things don't have to be big to be good. The concentration of great power at the top of government has not made our lives easier nor produced peace or any other desirable result. It is likely that the next decade will see even more political disintegration, which will be rendered harmless by an increase in economic integration. Prosperity and social progress can and do take place in small, independent states; they do not require a centralized, imperial framework. A good example is the nation of Finland, which successfully broke away from the Russian empire in 1917 and has managed to stay independent ever since. Today, Finland, a small nation with less than six million people, has become one of the more prosperous countries in Europe. There is no reason why other small countries, such as the Baltic states, the Ukraine, and for that matter, oppressed Asian countries such as Tibet, could not follow the example of Finland. Once the idol of bigness reveals itself to be yet another god that has failed, people will understand that any country, no matter how small or oppressed, can achieve sovereignty and prosperity.

The second development that is vitally involved in ushering in the new world order is the development of high technology. Technology is often regarded as a menace to individual freedom. The very word evokes thoughts of huge, impersonal and tyrannical corporations gobbling up individuals, businesses and countries. Many of us have seen movies in which mad computers want to take over. Hal in *2001* is but one example. While technology clearly has its shadow side, it is quite likely that the high-tech revolution of recent years will turn out to be a liberating force.

The industry of the past phase of civilization (sometimes called "low technology") was big industry, and bigness always implies oppressiveness. The new high technology, however, is not big in the same way. While the old technology produced and distributed material resources, the new technology produces and disseminates information. The resources marketed in high technology are less about matter and more about mind. Under the impact of high technology, the world is moving increasingly from a physical economy into what might be called a "metaphysical economy." We are in the process of recognizing that consciousness rather than raw materials or physical resources constitutes wealth.

No single development has facilitated this recognition as powerfully as the computer. The computer chip can be regarded as the grand symbol of the liberating technology that is currently emerging. A word processor disk, for instance, can be made from about ten cents worth of plastic and paper plus a few cents worth of other materials, though the program it contains may be worth hundreds of dollars. Thus a piece of computer software represents what could be called "metaphysical wealth." The smallness of the computer chip and the minimal amount of physical resources it takes to produce it symbolize the fact that civilization has moved from a big, heavy oppressive kind of technology to a small, mobile and above all consciousness-centered technology. This does not mean that the production and distribution of material resources is passé, but that the emphasis has shifted to another plane, or phase, as it were. Moreover, high technology is a powerful enemy of tyrants and bureaucrats. A "high tech"-oriented society does not oppress individuals; rather, it frees them from centralized control and bestows on them much power over their own destiny.

The last hopeful sign of change is the possibility of a

moral revival as part of the new trend of civilization. As the psychological center of gravity of the culture shifts from material resources to consciousness, it becomes ever more important to make sure that the quality of consciousness improves. A renewal of individual ethics can be seen in this context as an epiphenomenon of the transformation of consciousness. Renewal of individual values, moral education of the individual soul and personal standards of discipline are all part of the search for the greater kingdom within. A general moral revival will not result from indoctrination in the particular value system of any one religious or cultural tradition (see Chapters 2 and 4). In fact, informed suggestions put forward within the last few years indicate that spiritual philosophies and practices of the kind espoused by the present writer, including Jungian psychology, occult, theosophical, and Gnostic thought, have contributed significantly to the changes taking place in the former Soviet Union and other totalitarian countries. In an information age, the quality of our consciousness will affect our politics, our economy and indeed our future more than it has in the past.

Thomas Jefferson warned that "if a nation expects to be ignorant and free, in a state of civilization, it expects what never was, and never will be." The kind of freedom he advocated, like the one dawning on the horizon of the world today, was always more a function of what people knew than of what they owned. The greatest ignorance is ignorance of one's deeper, spiritual nature, as Jefferson and many other sages of the past realized. It is important, therefore, not to yield to the temptation to reduce the present alchemical changes in the world to the scale of mere economic dimensions. Free enterprise is an important aspect of freedom, and many of the woes of this century have resulted from its denigration.

Still, all freedoms depend on and are suspended from a deep, potent and all-important mystery. This mystery has been called by many names: God, the Spirit, Reality, the Good. It is this ultimate yet immediate mystery which Jung described in his *Seven Sermons to the Dead:* "To it goes the long journey of the soul. . . ; in it shine all things which otherwise might keep man from the greater world with the brilliance of a great light."

It may well be that, in earlier phases of the alchemical *opus*, this mystery could be approached primarily by way of faith. Today, faith has been replaced in many minds by what depth psychology calls consciousness, the same concept known to past ages as Gnosis. To "have faith in someone else's faith," as William James put it, is no longer satisfying for many.

We need to make sure that the current moral revival is part of an overall growth of human consciousness. In the earlier phases of the alchemy of this century, we forgot that material progress remains precarious without moral progress. Social policies were devised that claimed to be morally neutral or "value free," though it was subsequently discovered that these policies in turn were fraught with disastrous moral implications and consequences. It is clear that other ways need to be found today. Among these ways, we might seriously consider the way of Gnosis, as amplified by Jung's psychology. To call attention to this possibility and this hope is the main objective of this work.

Bibliography

Atwood, M. A. *Hermetic Philosophy and Alchemy*. 1850. Reprint. New York: Johnson Reprint Corp., 1967.

Augustine, Saint. *City of God*. Translated by Marcus Dods. New York: Random House, 1950.

Campbell, Joseph. *The Masks of God: Primitive Mythology*. New York: The Viking Press, 1959.

Edinger, Edward F. *The Creation of Consciousness: Jung's Myth for Modern Man*. Toronto: Inner City Books, 1984.

Eliade, Mircea. *The Forge and the Crucible*. Translated by Stephen Corrin. New York: Harper & Row, 1962.

_____ . *Shamanism: Archaic Techniques of Ecstasy*. New York: Pantheon, 1964.

Hall, Manly Palmer. *America's Assignment with Destiny*. Los Angeles: The Philosophical Research Society, 1951.

_____ . *The Secret Teachings of All Ages*. Los Angeles: The Philosophical Research Society, 1975.

Hayek, F. A. *The Constitution of Liberty*. Chicago: The University of Chicago Press, 1960.

Heard, Gerald. *The Third Morality*. New York: William Morrow & Co., 1937.

_____ . *Pain, Sex and Time*. New York: Harper & Brothers Publ., 1939.

_____. *Morals Since 1900.* London: Andrew Dakers Ltd., 1950.

Hoeller, Stephan A. *The Gnostic Jung and the Seven Sermons to the Dead.* Wheaton, IL: Theosophical Publishing House, 1982.

Johnson, William, ed. *Reflections on Faith and Freedom.* Los Angeles: Spiritual Mobilization, 1952.

Jung, C. G. *C. G. Jung Speaking.* Edited by William McGuire and R. F. C. Hull. Bollingen Series XCVII. Princeton, NJ: Princeton University Press, 1977.

_____. *Memories, Dreams, Reflections.* Edited by A. Jaffe. New York: Pantheon, 1963.

_____. *Psychological Types.* Collected Works Volume 6. Revised translation by R. F. C. Hull. Princeton University Press, 1971. From the Collected Works of C. G. Jung. Bollingen Series XX, R. F. C. Hull, trans. Sir Herbert Read, Michael Fordham, Gerhard Adler, eds. William McGuire, exec. ed.

_____. *Two Essays on Analytical Psychology.* Collected Works Volume 7. Princeton, NJ: Princeton University Press, 1966.

_____. *The Archetypes of the Collective Unconscious.* Collected Works Volume 9, i. Princeton, NJ: Princeton University Press, 1969.

_____. *Civilization in Transition.* Collected Works Volume 10. Princeton, NJ: Princeton University Press, 1970.

_____. *Psychology and Religion: West and East.* Collected Works Volume 11. Princeton, NJ: Princeton University Press, 1969.

_____. *Psychology and Alchemy.* Collected Works Volume 12. Princeton, NJ: Princeton University Press, 1968.

_____. *The Practice of Psychotherapy.* Collected

Works Volume 16. Princeton, NJ: Princeton University Press, 1966.

———. *The Development of Personality*. Collected Works Volume 17. Princeton, NJ: Princeton University Press, 1964.

Mises, Ludwig von. *Human Action, A Treatise on Economics*. New Haven: Yale University Press, 1949.

———. *Planning for Freedom and other Essays and Addresses*. South Holland, IL: Libertarian Press, 1952.

Neumann, Erich. *The Great Mother*. Translated by Ralph Mannheim. Bollingen Series XLVII. Princeton, NJ: Princeton University Press, 1963.

———. *The Origins and History of Consciousness*. Translated by R. F. C. Hull, Bollingen Series XLII. New York: Pantheon, 1954.

Odajnyk, Voladymyr Walter. *Jung and Politics: The Political and Social Ideas of C. G. Jung*. New York: Harper & Row, 1976.

Pagels, Elaine. *The Gnostic Gospels*. New York: Random House, 1979.

———. *Adam, Eve, and the Serpent*. New York: Random House, 1988.

Progoff, Ira. *Jung's Psychology and Its Social Meaning*. Garden City, NY: Anchor Press/Doubleday, 1973.

Robinson, James M., ed. *The Nag Hammadi Library in English*. Revised Edition. San Francisco: Harper & Row, 1988.

Shaffer, Butler D. *Calculated Chaos: Institutional Threats to Peace and Human Survival*. San Francisco: Alchemy Books, 1985.

Singer, June. *Androgyny, Toward a New Theory of Sexuality*. Garden City, NY: Anchor Press/Doubleday, 1976.

Weatherford, Jack. *Indian Givers: How the Indians of the Americas Transformed the World.* New York: Crown Publishers, 1989.

Yates, Frances A. *Giordano Bruno and the Hermetic Tradition.* Chicago: The University of Chicago Press, 1964.

_____. *The Rosicrucian Enlightenment.* London: Routledge & Kegan Paul, 1972.

INDEX

Abortion, 140; and birth control, 55
Adjustment, Freudian concept of, 90
Albertus Magnus, Saint, 157
Alchemical, mercury, 223; symbolism, 115; transformation, 221, 226; transformation of our civilization, 228; vessels, 211
Alchemists, 9, 31
Alchemy, 30, 121, 144, 150, 202, 216, 221-225; moral, 227; of this century, 232
Alcohol, 160
Alien God (*Deus Absconditus*), 173
Altering of consciousness, 158-159
America, 45, 50, 52; as extraverted, 49; as Hermetic vessel, xv, 116; religion in, 45
American, colonies, 45; Com-

munist movement, 165; psyche, 205, 208, 209
American Indians, 144
American Republic, 115; founders of, 64, 161, 168, 184; founding of, 170-171
American Revolution, 168
Androgyny, 212
Angébert, Jean-Michel, 101
Anima and Animus, 70-81, 211
Animal gods, 156
Apartheid, 177
Archaic spirituality, 155
Archetypal, forces, 110; heirophant, 151; images, 170; psyche, 210; Self, 70; symbols, 111, 134
Archetype, 73, 74, 77, 133; central, 69; collective unconscious, 124, 155; Great Devouring Mother, 55; Great Mother, 111, 124; Hermetic, 116; Jehovic, 39, 113; of Christ, 150; of Perfection,

237

QUEST BOOKS
are published by
The Theosophical Society in America,
Wheaton, Illinois 60189-0270,
a branch of a world organization
dedicated to the promotion of brotherhood and
the encouragement of the study of religion,
philosophy, and science, to the end that man may
better understand himself and his place in
the universe. The Society stands for complete
freedom of individual search and belief.
In the Classics Series well-known
theosophical works are made
available in popular editions.